# MUST. HAVE. WINE.

*A Toast to Motherhood*

Katrina Epp

Leah Speer

MUST. HAVE. WINE.

We support and encourage responsible drinking. While we enjoy wine, our commitment to being loving parents and role models for our children come first.

Copyright © 2012 by Must. Have. Wine., LLC

All rights reserved, including the right to reproduce this book or portions thereof in any form whatsoever.

MUST. HAVE. WINE.

www.must-have-wine.com

The names and other identifying details of some characters in this book have been changed.

EDITING BY CAROLE BELLACERA
WWW.CAROLEBELLACERA.COM

COVER DESIGNED BY LEAVEN MARKETING
WWW.LEAVENMARKETING.COM

Manufactured in the United States of America

ISBN-13: 978-0615716794

ISBN-10: 0615716792

*To our amazing **children** who lovingly and insanely inspired this book—you bring so much joy into our lives. We adore you!*

*And to our **husbands**—without your support, we never would have survived writing this book…or for that matter, motherhood!*

## *Acknowledgements*

## *Katrina Says Thanks*

I found writing this acknowledgment more difficult than writing the manuscript itself. How on Earth could I thank all the people that have been essential to me during this process? Instead, I'm going to name the people who have taken time out of their busy lives to make this book possible and hope *everyone* knows how much I appreciated their love and support during the last two years.

First and foremost, I have to thank God for giving me the gift of writing…for opening the right doors and closing the wrong ones. For loving *me*.

Secondly, I must thank my mother. She's been the rock that's kept me solid, and the strength pushing me to believe I was a writer, even before *I* believed it. She's a constant support system, no matter *what* I'm doing.

To my father, I say you've given me the world, and shown me what it means to *have* the world. You've shown me true drive, success, and how to get up after you fall, and how to keep getting up no matter who pushes you back down. I see you and my eyes shine with pride, dad. One is lucky to have parents like I've had.

To Tammy, thank you for sharing your stories and reading my articles, and just being a believer in this book from day one, I hope it makes you proud.

To Carole; without you, this would never be. Thank you for supporting me as a teacher, and as a friend. Thank you for seeing the amazing possibilities and therefore introducing me to your daughter Leah. And thank you for editing, believing and pushing this project with pride.

To Anna; our website design guru, thank you for seeing and helping execute our dream. You've been patient and awesome this entire process! Thank you! To our other design guru, Amber, you are brilliant and thank you for taking the cover and logo to the place it was meant to be.

To Lacy, without you, I wouldn't have had the confidence in my writing ability. You've been the force right behind my mother, telling me I will succeed at this. You read everything I write, and for that, I thank you. To Amber, thank you for reading (reading *every single thing*), commenting, and supporting me throughout this bumpy ride. I appreciated your honesty, your humor, your sarcasm, and always your wit. You are such a great friend and without you, this book wouldn't be the book it is. To Mandy, thank you for all the inspirational emails, following the blog, your true interest in our success, and the insight (and constant assistance) into your business savvy that will ultimately help us in building our brand. You've also had a large impact on Must. Have. Wine., in every sense. I love you girl. To Iryna, you are *amazing* my friend. Thank you for editing, critiquing, and supporting this project day in and day out. I think you've read every story, five times, in different ways. You've been a true follower to our blog and to our Anti-Chicken Fingers Movement and for that; I'll never forget your support. To Julia (and always mother Patty!) for reading and rating the manuscript, honestly. I appreciate your feedback and your listening ear, as always. You're the best! To Lindi and Shauna for supporting this process and always making sure *everyone* knows about our book and our blog. And, to all my other wonderful friends and family; I cannot name you all but I will tell you that I appreciate your support and love!

To Shannon; thank you for supporting me in this journey and making it possible for me to be able to work on this brand full-time. You've never questioned if I'd see success and I see the pride in your eyes when you talk about what I'm doing. You are the half that makes me whole—I love you!

To my babies Callie and Clayton. You've been as much a reason for me to do this as anything. I want to show you how to follow your dreams. To believe in yourself. To build an empire or a small city; whatever it is you desire. I love you both and can't wait to see you grow into the amazing young people I know you're destined to become.

To Leah; my amazing and brilliant writing partner. I know I'm a pain in the ass, and I know I can be a non-detail oriented perfectionist at times (an oxy-moron, I know…but that's me!). But, we balance each other well and I truly do consider this like a marriage. We're great together and I'm in this for the long haul. Thanks for committing so much time and effort into something we both believed in. True faith is believing in something you can't yet necessarily see. I have faith in you, in our partnership, and in our brand. Let's change the world, one book at a time. I love you!

To our dedicated and loyal followers; where would we be without you? Thank you for following the blog, trying out our recipes, commenting, and just showing your support in general.  We hope to keep you reading far into the future!

And last, but most certainly not least, to everyone who took the time to share their personal experiences—whether they are in this book or will be in one of the future editions; you are as crucial to our success as we are as the writers and we thank you from the bottom of our hearts.

*Acknowledgements*

*Leah Says Gracias*

I want to thank every single loyal follower out there. You are the ones who encouraged us to keep going, to keep writing, to keep growing. Thank you so much for all of your support and we hope you stay with us for the long haul!

I am one lucky girl! I am so blessed with many wonderful friends to turn to when I do need encouragement or a laugh. Not to mention, life wouldn't be nearly as fun without my *vintage* girls. And there is a little something about each of you that make my life better. For keeping me laughing since 1999, I thank and love Becky Ciletti…the funniest person in the world, in my opinion. To Susanne MacNicoll, my bestie from sophomore year of high school; these years of friendship have kept us near and far, yet through all of life's ups and downs, we've managed to stay so close. I appreciate you! To Mary Ann Bacurin, oh girl! It's always so fun hanging with you, flipping through our *People* magazines and talking about life. You do motherhood well and have answered my calls every single time I needed you. I love you! Beth Bryant, I knew I could count on you! Two of your stories are rocking these pages and you are one of the cover models for one of our chapter pages (with an endless amount of pics to choose from, thank you!). Dana Langfitt, you inspire me with how you handle being a working mom so seamlessly and I've mentioned you a few times in my stories for just that reason! Don't worry, Buffy-I wouldn't *not* mention you. You've brought us all endless good times. Jody, Jody, Jody Dianna. My buddy! So great chatting with you, especially recently. I count myself lucky I got to see you so much this year! And thank you for introducing Trina and I to the hilarious writings of Maggie McCallie, who offered her story "Giving My Kids the Sun, the Moon and the Stars." Officer Sara Kreger, thank you so much for inspiring a bedtime story that kept my boys happy and intrigued for at least six months and for being a friend for life!

Thank you Ricci Boyer for being an innovative photographer! You captured the essence of mom plus wine! And Tanya Sue Belew Spiller for letting Ricci handle your camera for such purposes. To Julie Hunsinger, Holly Murrell, and Katie Hagan for your undying enthusiasm and everlasting friendship that is only enhanced lakeside.

To the Real Housewives of Rho Omicron, you know who you are, you all made me realize from day one that I truly was not alone in this crazy world of motherhood. Our annual weekend retreat is a must for me and it always reinforces that we're all going through the same stuff and we are all great moms!

And all the AOPis that have ever lived! Especially, those Rho Omicron girls. Including Andrea Rizk, my sister from my MTSU days, who so kindly submitted the story Fire F*ck.

To my Baby Mamas from Nov 08 – how could I have survived pregnancy and the first years without you all! We've gone through so much together. Support and friendship from real *awesome* moms all over the country... I heart you! Thanks to Joanna Davis of joanna davis photography, for her story "Mommy, You Bad!"

I can't write a book and *not* mention the Bataran cousins who I am always thinking of, even if I can't chat with you like I used to in my sunny Southern California days. Erika, you introduced me to my husband and without him, I wouldn't have these amazing kids who inspired this book. I adore you! Meagan, you know you had your part in that as well and kept those times so fun. Which leads me to Kelly Francois, who is dearly loved and thought of often even across the miles.

To Andrew Rhodes, who has stayed in touch with me all of these years - from the young career girl in New York City through a bunch of moves to becoming a mommy of two. Andrew, you are someone I consider a good friend for life.

To all the contributors of this book – you made it amazing. We truly couldn't have written this without your stories! Since some of you want to remain anonymous, we thank each of you, from the bottom of our heart.

To Anna Kaiser for your patience in working with two writers on designing our website.

To Amber Chancey for being our angel – swooping in at the exact moment we needed you and designing a book cover we are so very proud of.

To Laura Munson who recommended we build a platform and to just write, write and write. And we have, so thank you! And on a side note, thank you for your book which made my marriage even stronger just as we started to write this book.

To Bethenny Frankel who seriously changed our lives in your books *A Place of Yes* and *Naturally, Thin*.

To Ama and Poppy, Aunt Mere, Aunt Jen and the cousins who make my boys so very happy: AJ, Tadan, Jake, Josh, Jesse, and Sayre.

To Gram and Uncle Dick in Denver. My boys (all three of them!) delight in your weekly phone conversations. We love you with all of our hearts! Go Broncos!

To my family who doesn't live so close, but stays very close in my heart: Uncle Charley, Aunt Suann, Gina Rose, Andrew, Aunt Michelle, Uncle Jim, Amanda and the coolest high school dude ever – CJ Weiman. And my grandparents who had a huge hand in who I am today, I wish I could still visit you for Sundays and meatballs.

To my Aunt Kathy who we wish were at more family affairs, and know you will be one day. We love you!

To my "big" baby brother, Uncle Stephen, who has been my constant in this crazy world of moving around and change. You're always there, no matter where I go or what I do. I love you so much!

Mom. Your incredible talent matched with your tenacity in this business of writing has encouraged me to never give up. And I'm not ever going to give up. This is just the beginning and I owe it to you! Dad. Your faith in me keeps the fire burning to do more and be better. You always taught that I have Bellacera in my blood and to go after my dreams…and I'm not going to stop! I love you both so much!

Zac, I remember the night I told you I wanted to write. You smiled and simply said, "I knew it all along." You felt the passion and encouraged me through many, many late nights and very early mornings, even waved at the door with naked boys by your side, as I drove off to the coffee shop to write in quiet. You make me better. Better. You are my real prince charmin'! I love you, babe!

Luke, my first born, you were the inspiration for many of these stories. You motivate me to work hard so that I could teach you that with determination and hard work, you can reach your dreams. I love you all the way to the moon and back. Zealand, my baby, you have taught me to never sweat the small stuff. Your smile brightens my heart *and an entire room*; I can honestly say, there is hardly a moment you don't have that huge gorgeous smile on your face! I love you baby, I'll always protect you.

This entire book would not have been possible without Katrina Epp, the other half of Must. Have. Wine., my writing partner and friend. We realized quickly we made the perfect team. We even got comfortable enough to get mad at one another and get over it. That is a true friend. Is it true we have *never ever* met in person? It's hard to believe because I feel like we've been sharing a glass of wine and conversation for years now. *Skype doesn't count!* I look forward to meeting you in the most awesome, mind-blowing moment we've only dreamt about. We've got it made friend! I love you, my Colorado sister!

Thank you God for blessing me in so many ways; with a passion for writing, and such amazing good friends and family. Amen…and Cheers!

*"guilt to motherhood

is like grapes to wine"*

~ Fay Weldon

# Table of Contents

| | |
|---|---|
| **INTRODUCTION** | **1** |

---

| | |
|---|---|
| **CHAPTER 1: CHIANTI** | **3** |
| *WHEN YOU NEED TO BE* **INSPIRED** | |

---

**Reason #1** — 5
I *am* a good mother! Cheers!

**Reason #2** — 7
Becoming a mom has made me lose my mind…literally!

**Reason #3** — 10
I finally figured out that I only have to be the mother I was made to be.

**Reason #4** — 13
I feel guilty, no matter what I do!

**Reason #5** — 16
I gave in to the French fry and chicken finger madness…after swearing I never would.

**Reason #6** — 19
I continue to set unreasonable expectations for myself…and therefore I often fail.

**Reason #7** — 21
I didn't expect this to be *this* challenging!

Must. Have. Wine.

**Reason #8** 23
I haven't slept in a week!

**Reason #9** 25
I'm ashamed at how shallow I could be…

**Reason #10** 28
I fight the battle every day to not give my child the same body image issues I've lived with my entire life.

**Reason #11** 31
I should've trusted my gut.

**Reason #12** 33
I'm going to have to let my baby go…one day.

**Reason #13** 34
I've had to learn the hard way that assuming anything regarding motherhood will backfire!

**Reason #14** 36
I'm scared I'm not living up the promises I've made to my children.

---

## CHAPTER 2: RIESLING 39

*WHEN YOU NEED TO BE* **AMUSED**

---

**Reason #15** 41
I couldn't save my son from that evil McDonald's slide.

**Reason #16** 43
Did she just ask about his penis? OMG, she did!

## Table of Contents

**Reason #17**     44
How am I supposed to know everything?

**Reason #18**     47
Yes, they really *are* paying attention!

**Reason #19**     48
Sometime you just have to work with what you've got!

**Reason #20**     50
Oops! Guess I better watch what I say!

**Reason #21**     51
Well, now that I'm totally embarrassed once again…

**Reason #22**     52
Everyone at church just heard him say the F word…everyone!

**Reason #23**     53
Pee, poop and spit up - all at once. Good times!

**Reason #24**     55
I dreamed of raising a soccer or basketball star…yeah, not so much.

**Reason #25**     58
Just experienced the most embarrassing moment at my pediatrician's office.

**Reason #26**     59
The things we get to hear come out of our children's mouths!

Must. Have. Wine.

**Reason #27**   60
You can't make this stuff up!

**Reason #28**   61
There's a little competition in this mama!

---

## CHAPTER 3: PINOT NOIR   **63**

*When you need to be* **encouraged**

---

**Reason #29**   65
As moms, we survive through our strength.

**Reason #30**   69
After months of fighting, our baby is finally declared healthy and disease free.

**Reason #31**   71
I never thought I'd recover from the loss…but that was before I saw all I was to gain.

**Reason #32**   73
We had to take our first trip to the ER.

**Reason #33**   76
How do I explain death to my baby?

**Reason #34**   79
I just dropped my baby off at daycare for the first time…and my heart is broken.

**Reason #35**   82
My child encouraged me to be brave.

# Table of Contents

**Reason #36**     85
I survived three months of constant crying, I can survive anything!

**Reason #37**     87
I don't want to go home to my crying newborn…

**Reason #38**     90
I do realize how blessed I truly am.

---

## CHAPTER 4: MOSCATO D'ASTI     93

*WHEN YOU NEED TO BE* **DELIGHTED**

---

**Reason #39**     95
I'm pretty sure everyone has seen or touched my boobs now…

**Reason #40**     98
Potty training success: check!

**Reason #41**     99
Our children are designed to be just who they are going to be…even at a very early age.

**Reason #42**     101
Score! My son likes the ladies!

**Reason #43**     103
Boys will be boys!

**Reason #44**     104
I have created a high-maintenance four-year-old.

Must. Have. Wine.

**Reason #45** — 106
Our family secret was revealed!

**Reason #46** — 108
Thank God, he didn't start a fire. *This time.*

**Reason #47** — 109
My kid tells it like it is, even when it's bossing her parents around.

**Reason #48** — 111
Mommy was put in time out today!

**Reason #49** — 112
My daughter + drama = I deserve that glass of wine, bitches!

**Reason #50** — 114
My reality as a mom is much different than I'd pictured.

## CHAPTER 5: SHIRAZ — 117

*WHEN YOU NEED TO BE* **RELIEVED**

**Reason #51** — 119
I had to call in sick today because I couldn't get my kids out the door.

**Reason #52** — 121
It's *my* turn to have a tantrum!

**Reason #53** — 124
The public tantrums are the worst! Could our children embarrass us more?

## Table of Contents

**Reason #54**      126
Is this why my husband calls me crazy?!

**Reason #55**      129
I feel resentment and annoyance toward my precious newborn.

**Reason #56**      131
Can a mommy get a break, *pleeease*!

**Reason #57**      134
I'm hungry, tired and I need to relax.

**Reason #58**      136
I gave into sex after an exhausting day and it better pay off!!

**Reason #59**      138
This isn't how I pictured it...at all!

**Reason #60**      141
I feel the darkness of motherhood enveloping me.

**Reason #61**      143
My child is manipulating me, yet again.

**Reason #62**      145
My child will not go the F*ck to sleep!

**Reason #63**      147
What happened to good babysitters?

**Reason #64**      150
I had to fly on a plane with my two young kids...alone.

Must. Have. Wine.

**Reason #65** — 153
I survived being stuck in traffic with two young kids.

**Reason #66** — 155
I can't believe some mothers…or their spoiled-rotten kids. Really?

**Reason #67** — 158
You try taking two kids under the age of three into a public bathroom!

**Reason #68** — 160
My kids are attached to me almost 14 hours a day, literally!

---

## CHAPTER 6: WHITE ZINFANDEL — **163**

*WHEN YOU NEED TO BE* **INDULGED**

---

**Reason #69** — 165
We just had the best day together!

**Reason #70** — 167
I wish I could turn back time…

**Reason #71** — 168
Memories made today will never be forgotten!

**Reason #72** — 170
There's nothing like sibling rivalry…except sibling love.

**Reason #73** — 172
Bedtime prayers can be so sweet…and sometimes funny.

# Table of Contents

**Reason #74**      174
There are no worries, just ask your toddler!

**Reason #75**      175
I'm amazed that such a young being can understand the importance of giving!

**Reason #76**      176
I wish I could take their pain away, but I can't this time.

**Reason #77**      178
I couldn't even get mad, it was so funny!

**Reason #78**      180
Plain brilliance coming out of my kid…

**Reason #79**      182
I did a lot of things wrong as a mother, but somehow this turned out right.

**Reason #80**      184
My kids napped today – Victory!

**Reason #81**      186
These are the moments where we realize how lucky we are to be moms.

**The Story of Katrina and Leah**      189

**Meet Katrina**      190

**Meet Leah**      191

## Introduction

Somehow we've bought into the idea that we need to be June Cleaver running this marathon of motherhood in heels and a frilly apron. I don't know about you, but I have shin splints from those damn heels!

The following are everyday stories from real moms that remind us we're all in this crazy race together, nobody is perfect, and other moms have been where we are. Let's sit together over our favorite bottle of wine and share in the ups and downs of this wondrous and challenging role we're all living.

# chapter 1

**complex & bold**
*chianti*
will complement this collection of stories that
**inspire**

Motherhood is complex. We are challenged every day to be the face of perfection for our children and the world. Let us be bold and inspire one another through the mommy guilt, imperfections, and emotional swells we all experience, just as the strong flavors of this dry red often lifts us with the hint of fruit.

www.must-have-wine.com

# Reason #1 • I *am* a good mother! Cheers!

## The Good Mother

*Does it make me a bad mom because I wish it were bedtime already?? Or at least time to cook dinner, so I can pour that glass of wine, hoping my husband keeps the kids entertained long enough for me to unwind, at least a little. Maybe this weekend I can get out for a bit. I haven't had a girls' night in forever and all I want is to get away for a few hours. No one tugging on my pant leg, no "mommy this" or "mommy that"… just a few drinks, appetizers, and some adult conversation.*

As much as we all want to be perfect and strive to be good mothers, we often feel as though we're failing. A *good* mother wouldn't fantasize about locking herself in her closet with a bottle of wine just to get some peace and quiet. A *good* mom wouldn't count the minutes until nap-time, begging for a break from her children. A *good* mom wouldn't dream of a getaway with her friends, desperate for some alone time *away* from her family. But the truth is–that's exactly what good mothers think. *Good* moms deserve a break.

The problem is…we don't know we're good mothers. We don't even know what a good mother is. Good moms *do* have breakdowns and snap at their kids. We crave a night out, if not to enjoy a bottle of wine with girlfriends, at least to have ice cream and watch a chick flick. Some days we give in and turn on cartoons for more than the appropriate amount of time just so we can get stuff done. We give our kids junk food as bribery. We dream about the days we'll give up diapers and bottles, because in some far-off land, we know

Must. Have. Wine.

freedom awaits us again, even though we know when those days come…we'll miss *this*.

Thinking nap-time is the highlight of most of your days doesn't make you a bad mom, because you're aware of it. Because you feel guilt for thinking it or admitting it. It makes you a good mom, because you *care*. The bad moms are the ones who *don't* care. They don't feel guilty when they don't take their kids to the park. They aren't concerned if their kids eat corndogs or McDonald's seven days a week. They don't need a break, because they aren't involved or interacting enough with their children in the first place. They aren't asking themselves whether they are a good mom or a bad mom because they simply *don't care*.

You *do* care! So smile, relax and enjoy nap-time. Have that glass of wine, guilt-free. Let go! Get dressed up and go out with your girlfriends and admit to your faults. Talk about your parenting imperfections and laugh over your mistakes. Together, by sharing stories and encouraging one another, we'll begin to understand what it truly means to be a good mother–what we're each uniquely destined to become and most times…already *are*.

# Reason #2 • Becoming a mom has made me lose my mind…literally!

## Today's Forecast: Scattered Mom Likely

**A peek inside the frenzied mind of an every day mom.**

Ah, my coffee. We're almost out of Splenda. I'm going to have to remember to put that on my grocery list. In fact, I need to make a run to Target today. Let me start a list. Where's the paper? I thought I'd just put it in this drawer yesterday.

*What do you need, baby? We're having breakfast in about 10 minutes, just let me finish cutting these grapes.* Should I cut these grapes in fourths? I'm going to just cut them all up now and then we'll be good to go the rest of the week. Oh, yeah, my coffee. We've got plenty of cream to last the next week or two; that's groovy. Love to my dad for giving us a whole bag of his home-roasted Kona coffee beans. That reminds me, I need to send him a thank you card. I wonder if I have any cards left over from the last bunch I bought. I'll have to remember to look for one later before I head over to the store.

*No, you may not have any chocolate. If you eat your breakfast, I'll think about giving you some chocolate milk.* Waffles! I wonder if I should just go ahead and make a waffle for myself? I know I was going to try and eat healthier today and scramble up some egg whites, but this will save me time on cooking and dishes and well…it's just easier. What the heck, right? I'll make it up at lunch time with a salad. I'm going to have to buy some fresh spinach though because I think what's left in

Must. Have. Wine.

the fridge is bad. As always, I'm awful at letting vegetables spoil. I know it drives Zac crazy. Why isn't my dear husband up yet?

*What happened to your clothes, young man? You're supposed to go on a doggie walk with your daddy and I just got you dressed! Go grab your undies!* There's Zac. Good! I'll get five, or maybe ten minutes of quiet while he takes the boys and our dog for their morning walk.

I cherish these peaceful minutes. I'll check my e-mail once they leave. I can start breakfast as soon as they get back. I also need to look up our play date for today; I can't remember if it's at 3:00 or 3:30. I hope it's at 3:30; that always gives us – *okay, bye, have fun. Be safe!* – wait…what was I just thinking? Oh, I can't remember. Doesn't matter anyway, I guess. I have to go potty. Did I just say potty in my head?

First, let me check my bank account to see if my paycheck went through. I also need to make sure my wallet is in my diaper bag before I leave this morning. Okay, good! It's there. I better go ahead and throw a few diapers in as well. I'm pretty sure I also have to pick some of those up at the store.

List! I've got to start a list. Finally! Here's some paper. Milk. Maybe a thank you card. Waffles. Diapers for my little ZZ. What was I going to have for lunch today? Oh, yeah, a salad. Spinach. I think I have everything else I need for lunch here. I could use some more Cherry Coke Zero. Wasn't there something else?

I check online and see my paycheck went through. I have spending money again! Good…because Luke's birthday will be here before we know it. What kind of party should we have? *Hey! You're back! That was fast!* What happened to my quiet time? I didn't get anything accomplished. Now I won't have another moment of quiet until nap-time and I'm not sure I can make that happen since ZZ woke up an hour before his brother. I must try! I'll go to the grocery store right before lunch time and keep him awake!

*Honey, what would you like from the store?* I hope my two favorite plates for the boys are clean. They are not in the cabinet where they should be. Not in the dishwasher. Now I know what my mom was talking about when she'd say she was losing her mind when we were little, because things weren't where she'd left them.

*Honey, where are the boys' blue and green plates?* Ha, there they are! I must've mindlessly grabbed them earlier when I first got to the kitchen. I can't believe they are sitting here right in front of me. *Here you go boys–a waffle, grapes and yogurt.* It feels so good to sit down. My boys are so sweet. It looks like they're hungry, too, which is always a good thing. You know what would be perfect right now? My coffee–which I haven't touched since I poured it an hour ago. Now where the heck is it?

Must. Have. Wine.

# Reason #3 • I finally figured out that I only have to be the mother I was made to be.

## Finding My Own Identity as a Mother

There's definitely a level of perfection we must strive towards as mommies. There's this quiet competition amongst us that we all know about…yet none of us actually talk about.

*How much did Sam weigh at his nine-month check-up? Oh really? Brandon is at the top of the chart as far as height. He's going to be so tall!*

*Sally's talking? Well, Kara has been saying full sentences for about six months now! We work with her every night. Oh, and Bailey is reading at a second grade reading level, and she's only five!*

Reading it, you realize how ridiculous it sounds. Yet, these are the conversations we have with one another every day. This, in turn, has us doing just about everything to ensure we aren't the mothers with the children who're left behind. I realized soon after having my first child that I wasn't like most mothers. I have ADHD, so my attention span was shorter than either of my toddler's. I have OCD as well, so if there's a sink full of dishes….it's nearly enough to send me over the edge. This already put me behind everyone else, at least in my own eyes.

I remember my sister telling me she spent an hour each night working with her daughter on letters and reading. So, of course, my niece was reading and writing before any other kids I knew. I felt guilty because I realized the only structure I'd set up like that at my house was reading a book before bedtime. I was far too busy between working full-time, commuting, and cooking a healthy meal every night to work in another hour of *anything*.

I felt terrible! My children were going to be behind in school! What if by not nurturing their precious brains, I'd actually held them back from future achievements? I thought this over for a few weeks. Maybe I needed to quit work. Maybe I needed to take medicine so I could be calmer and more focused at home. Maybe I needed to Google some home lesson plans we could implement into our nightly schedule.

One day after rushing both children to different places early in the morning so I could make a staff meeting, it finally occurred to me—my sister is a stay-at-home mom. She doesn't work, nor does she have to commute anywhere. Her sole focus is her children and she loves that. But I pride myself in my work. I have to have my own identity as a professional and I like being able to take my family on fun vacations, or buy things when we need them and not have to think twice.

If I stayed home, I'd be crazy–and I'd drive them crazy. That's why I pay for an expensive, yet amazing preschool…because I don't have the patience to sit through a lesson plan each night. Plus, I think how scary it would be if I was in charge of teaching my child anything educational. My mind jumps from one subject to another, rarely thinking in a normal order of steps or workflow. While I may not be able to be Super Mom when it comes to home lesson plans, I do have great things to offer them. I cook well. I can find pride in the fact I cook healthy meals each night for my family. I take time to ensure each meal is balanced with lean meats, proteins, whole grain or whole wheat, and a fruit or veggie. And, of course, I smother them with affection.

Must. Have. Wine.

  Looking at other moms shouldn't make us competitive, but rather, give us clarity on why being different in the way we all approach parenting works for each of us.  It's taken some time, but I've finally figured out it really doesn't matter who's reading first, or who's growing the tallest.  It doesn't matter if you are a working or a stay-at-home mom.  It doesn't matter if you cook every night, or order takeout.  You have to invent a life and identity as a mom that works for you, and your family.  Perfection is in the eyes of the beholder…so let's support one another in all creating our own.

Chapter 1: Stories That Inspire

# Reason #4 • I feel guilty, no matter what I do!

## Guilt Will Always Be There–
## Let Love Triumph!

"Stay at home or work. It really doesn't matter *what* you do. You'll find a way to feel guilty about something either way. You just have to do what feels right to you and what works best for your family," explains a wise and dear friend of mine. As we chat on the phone, I'm staring out at the Space Needle from my luxurious, very quiet (*aaah, I remember quiet*) hotel room, rubbing my almost eight-months-pregnant belly.

At the time, I wanted nothing more than to be a stay-at-home mom. It had been my dream, even after ten years of exciting business trips and extravagant meals at the best restaurants across the country. But there didn't seem to be a practical way to make it work with one salary and two mortgages. Yet, it made me feel better simply by hearing my old friend, a college sorority sister who I've always respected and seems to do motherhood seamlessly as a successful working mom, tell me that *all* moms feel guilty about something some of the time.

Three years and two toddlers later, as a work-at-home-mom, I now know this to be true. No matter what you try to do right for your family or your children (*or yourself*), guilt will sneak its way in. These are just *some* of the ways guilty mom syndrome kicks in:

Must. Have. Wine.

## The Working Mom

**Her early morning thoughts.** Today, I'm going to be the best mom ever! I'm going to work hard today to teach my kids how successful you can be in life; while also making money so we can have what we need to live comfortably, and hey, even a Disney Vacation or two.

**Her guilt.** I should be home with my kids doing crafts, flipping through sight words index cards, taking them to the park, making them a healthy, home-cooked lunch and kissing them at nap-time.

## The Stay-At-Home Mom

**Her early morning thoughts.** Today, I'm going to be the best mom ever! I'm going to spend so much one-on-one time with my children today and give them love and affection, teach them about the world, and make a craft out of autumn leaves and paint. We'll run around the house, laughing the day away. I will make them a healthy, home-cooked lunch before I kiss them at nap-time.

**Her guilt.** I don't have time to cook these kids a healthy, home-cooked lunch…there are toys all over this place, paint all over the table and chairs, and I can't even get them to sit still for one minute to do our flash cards. What if I'm playing with them too much and they won't learn how to play independently? I feel so guilty for wanting it to be nap-time!

## The Work-At-Home Mom

**Her early morning thoughts.** Today, I'm going to be the best mom ever! I'm going to balance playing with my kiddos and working on my business plan. I'll take some time to prepare a healthy, home-cooked lunch and snuggle with them before their two-hour nap. During nap-time, I'll get in a few solid hours of work. After nap-time, I'll let them run around during a park play date.

**Her guilt.** I just spent thirty minutes playing doctor and being locked up in jail. I painted with them earlier today. We're going to the playground after nap-time. Yet, I feel bad when I do steal a few minutes to get on my laptop. Sometimes I can get up to 15 minutes; the rest of the time I feel like I'm neglecting them since I'm not playing with them 24/7. I swear, they'd be happier in preschool, learning and playing with other kids. The day is ticking by and if I want to get any work done, we'll have to settle for Spaghetti Os for lunch. I guess I can still get some work done during nap-time, and there is always after bedtime.

So, there it is, Moms– guilt in its finest. You can try to do the right thing and be the best mom ever, but there is always a flip-side to the picture. You're either doing too much or too little. Instead of getting swept up in all the things we can't do or control, let the simple, beautiful moments—the ones that *really* matter, slay the guilt. When your child walks into the room and they can see the sparkle in your eyes that you're truly happy to see them, the attention you give them when they're holding that invisible microphone and shaking their groove thing for their favorite audience, when they can feel your love as you hold them tight at night reading them their last bedtime story; with each kiss and *I love you* whispered in their ear.

Guilt will always be there…let love triumph!

## Reason #5 • I gave in to the French fry and chicken finger madness… after swearing I never would.

### Fast Food Snobbery

Before I had children, I'd look at moms feeding their precious young children French fries and processed chicken nuggets, and pompously nudge my friends, outwardly judging these horrible moms for putting the fast food poison into their pure and developing babes. "I can promise you this—I will not take my child to a fast food restaurant. I just don't want them growing up eating that type of food!"

Then I got pregnant. I stayed clear of caffeine, sushi, and soft cheeses. Of course, alcohol was non-existent, *almost*. I did have a wine cooler on my birthday in my third trimester. I exercised through the first half of my pregnancy, but admittedly, also indulged in late-night root beer floats with my husband regularly. I was still drinking tons of water and making sure I was eating plenty of greens to help my unborn baby thrive.

When my son was born, I proudly breastfed. I worked full-time and pumped religiously in a small bathroom in the office building where I worked. When it came time to start baby foods, I let myself down a little when I decided against processing the health food from home. However, I got over it and found myself challenged to search through the array of tiny jars for a balanced diet of veggies, fruits and grains.

I found out I was pregnant again when my son was only six months old. At that point, I stopped breastfeeding and switched him to formula. As the months went by, I was excited about the pending birth of our second child and continued to take care of myself, however, occasionally giving into a bit of fast food to ease my hectic lifestyle. I was somehow able to convince myself that a *chicken* biscuit for breakfast was way healthier than a sausage biscuit.

In January, we welcomed the newest member of our family and breastfeeding was again, my priority. Two days out of the week, we were lucky enough to have my husband home with the boys. I remember the first time I called home to check on them and my husband proudly announced our 15-month-old had just enjoyed his first hot dog ("dog-dog" as my son would soon call it). I was horrified. First of all, hot dogs are the worst thing to give a toddler when it comes to choking hazards. Secondly, that is *so* not on our list of healthy foods! I kept it cool though and reminded him that the bites should be cut up in the tiniest of slices, if he should desire to serve that to our child again. *Sweetly*. Not too long after that, I'd returned home from work to hear the recap of the day including a road trip through the Wendy's drive-thru.

"He loves French fries!" My husband joyously announced.

*My dreams!* My dreams of my children not experiencing the fast food evil had crashed right before my eyes.

Fast forward to a life with two toddlers. I'm now a stay-at-home mama and I engage my boys in endless play dates, usually 20 minutes away. Many scenarios find me racing home and trying to keep them awake before nap-time. The perfect solution—waffle fries and chicken nuggets. It keeps them awake the whole ride home and the extra bonus—no preparation involved. After an afternoon at the aquarium when their dad is working late, the beauty in the thought of no dishes to clean up after dinner wins, and I pull into a drive-thru. I swear I can get my kids to eat more while

Must. Have. Wine.

strapped in their car seat than I can get them to eat at the table at home. To ease my guilt a little, many of the fast food restaurants offer apple slices and I've been able to swap out the fries *some* of the time.

# Reason #6 • I continue to set unreasonable expectations for myself…and therefore I often fail.

## Unreasonable Expectations

How did I picture preschool for my child? Just like everything else, I imagine. All happy-go-lucky, with roses and sugar-coated cherries on top. Don't we all picture our children's lives this way? Perfect. We are going to be the best parents, have the smartest children, the greatest home lives. And then, when reality hits, we don't know what went wrong.

I dropped Callie off for her first day of preschool with a grin on my face and a tear in my eye. *How did we get here already?* That afternoon I got a follow-up letter when I picked her up telling me how wonderful my little girl was and how much happiness and enthusiasm she contributed to the group. A mental check mark in my brain as an early parenting success scored.

Weeks later I learned that Callie was having a few issues. Her pretty blonde teacher met me at the door with an optimistic smile on her face that could only mean trouble. The way she started was classic: "Callie is such an addition to our group; so charming and full of life…but…you should know there are some things we're working on."

She proceeded to tell me in a no-less-bubbly manner that my daughter was having some trouble listening, and had been caught telling a lie, as well as stealing. Already, a young criminal on my hands.

Must. Have. Wine.

  I drove home in tears. My terrible parenting had surely led to a future drug-abuser, jail-bird, schizophrenic, and possibly even worse. What was I to do?

  After sifting through my self-loathing party, a good friend convinced me that stealing a sea shell and lying by saying she didn't hit a boy wouldn't deem my daughter a future sociopath or drug dealer. She was simply like all other typical four-year-olds…she was finding herself and learning about the do's and don'ts of toddlerhood. Just because I'd let her watch too many episodes of **SpongeBob**, and even **Jurassic Park** in her dinosaur-loving days…didn't mean I was a terrible parent.

  I think the dreams we let ourselves strive towards as parents are what sets us up for failure. When we don't reach the impossible goals we've set when raising our little ones, we automatically are plagued by guilt and assume every small failure our children face is that of our own mistakes and parenting mishaps.

  Callie is now thriving in preschool. It took some time, but we eventually worked past the small issues she was having and have since moved on. I've realized…she's only four. We're going to have *many* more hurdles in the future!

Chapter 1: Stories That Inspire

# Reason #7 • I didn't expect this to be *this* challenging!

## Expect the Unexpected

I didn't plan on having children. I loved and enjoyed having them around, however, my husband and I were too selfish at that time in our lives, and knew it wouldn't be the responsible thing to do.

Then one day, *surprise*! We were pregnant, even after taking the appropriate measures to ensure that wouldn't happen. I had a few meltdowns…though it didn't take long for me to see the positive, and I immediately began to prepare for motherhood.

I'm very structured. I like to know what to expect, and when. I don't like surprises, and I don't like the *unknown*. I started watching shows on TV that pertained to parenthood. I sucked in all the knowledge I could with the thought that when my little baby boy came, we'd be prepared.

When Kesel James was born, there was no way I could be prepared for that special little boy, or the love I felt for him. We may not have wanted children, but this little angel filled my heart with joy and brought tears to my eyes. No one could've truly expressed the emotions you feel toward your newborn baby.

As the weeks wore on after we came home, I realized again that nothing could've gotten me ready for the craziness that ensued. Sure, everyone tells you to expect to get zero sleep. They warn you to expect to have a crying baby that can't tell you what he needs, and to know you aren't going to be able to control every aspect of this particular situation, no matter how hard you try.

Nobody mentioned it would take me over an hour just to prepare for as mundane a task as simply going to the grocery store. And that's *just* for getting the diaper bag and Kesel ready. Packing diapers, formula, and an extra outfit just in case…all this for just a trip to the store! No one said that the minute I'd think I was ready and would head out the door; he'd poop or spit up all over himself, causing me to turn around and start the darned process all over again.

I also wasn't warned that one of the perils of motherhood was car rides. It takes a while to get used to getting your baby *in* the car seat—as well as *used* to the car seat. For a new mother, a 15-minute ride to the store may take 45 minutes or more by the time you stop, find the pacifier, and soothe him…is he hungry again? Honestly, I don't know how breastfeeding mamas do it!

Then you get to the store–that's an entirely new battle zone. You're trying not to imagine all the germs around you as the person next to the produce aisle coughs or wheezes. You try not to stare at the dirty little boy with grimy hands touching everything in sight, infecting it all with any sort of bacteria he may have on him. The shopping process takes what would usually be an hour or less—twice as long because, again, you're soothing, feeding, changing diapers…whatever it takes to keep this little being from wailing and disrupting the entire store, as well as your sanity.

By the time you're home, especially the first time, you swear you'll never do it again. Until the next time. Nobody can even begin to heed warnings on all the craziness of being a new mother…it's just best to brace yourself for the bumpy ride and take on the challenges as they come.

Chapter 1: Stories That Inspire

# Reason #8 • I haven't slept in a week!

## Mommies Need Sleep, Too!

I cried out loud in sync with my one-year-old who was weeping desperately. It's early March and a new round of colds has found their way into our home, attacking my husband and two-year-old first before it took hold of my baby. Funny how I always dodge these things but somehow still feel the effects...

I'm exhausted! The kind of exhausted where you pass a mirror and don't recognize who's looking back at you. The kind of exhausted where your educated mind truly can't reason the possibility that you will *ever* find sleep again. The kind of tired where your tears actually burn your eyes, begging to *please* shut them tight.

My husband's snoring had kept me up earlier in the week, followed by a couple of nights spent waking up every hour to care for my coughing and wheezing toddler. With him finally sleeping through the night again, I am now on night two with my baby boy who seems to have gotten the worst of it.

So here I am. Almost a week with just a few hours of sleep each night. How is it that I have the energy to rock my son, hold him tight through his tears, and comfort him when I feel like my body is about to shut down. I try everything...and nothing works.

An hour has gone by and finally, his eyes close as he rapidly sucks in the last of his throbbing sobs. I start to relax. My shoulders settle into the couch, my back following suit as I breathe a sigh and my eyes roll back in my head...then like a

Must. Have. Wine.

black cat jumping out from behind a plant in a 1970s horror flick, his sudden cry tenses my whole being. But his eyes are still closed and his sobs taper off. His chest peacefully rises and falls to the rhythm of relief. I start to sob; muffling every sound with my pillow. Looking at the clock, I know even if I did fall asleep now, my older son will be awake in two hours just as my husband heads off to work.

I wasn't going to make it! Isn't this how the strongest of mothers break?

I pull myself up and go to the window. The moonlight shines a message of comfort to me. I can't be alone in this. There has got to be another mother out there going through the same exact thing. Another mother lying awake somewhere, wishing she could just get some sleep.

And then I realize…these are the moments that make us mothers. It's not just that first step, or the first smile, or even the first word. It's the first tooth and soothing your baby through that terrible pain. It's the first real cold, and the helplessness you feel as you try to do everything you can to make them feel better. It's the endless string of sleepless nights you endure, all because you are a mother. It's the grit, the tears and the heartache we feel because we love these little beings more than ourselves. That's what makes us true mothers. It's what makes it possible to appreciate the wonderful times. Without these moments, none of the good would be earned.

I look over at my son perfectly nestled on our couch, and fall on the opposite sofa, finally letting sleep overcome me.

Chapter 1: Stories That Inspire

# Reason #9 • I'm ashamed at how shallow I could be...

## Pink or Blue...I Love You

"Well, what if we have a boy?" My husband asked one day.

I pondered this for only a second. Not possible! What would I do with a boy? They were everything I'd had nightmares about—boogers, burping, and other disgusting behaviors. Nope, I was going to have a girl!

I never wanted children, *necessarily*. I was far too selfish...and far too vain. I loved my body and there wasn't anything that would make me want to ruin it the way I'd seen so many mothers do by having children.

I was afraid of the poopy diapers, the snotty noses, the sleepless nights...none of it sounded appealing to me. So, you can only imagine my lack of glee when my husband announced that he was ready to have a baby. Of course, I think we all compromise with our spouses on one thing or another; this was just a little too big to swallow.

After a ton of coaxing from him, and of course, from both of our families, I started considering it. I slowly adapted to the possibility one day I could be curling my future daughter's hair, or buying her clothes. We could shop together, go to the bookstore together...we could do everything together. Suddenly, the idea seemed a whole lot more reasonable.

I studied the internet and books for hours. I wanted to know the statistics for having girls from family trees to sex

Must. Have. Wine.

positions—I was going to do whatever it took. Even the Chinese calendar which predicts the sex of your baby wasn't too far-fetched for me.

I followed all the instructions, all the tips…all the advice. And after getting pregnant on the first try, I could already feel the itch to start buying clothes. *Pink* clothes.

I was so anxious, I almost didn't make it to 20 weeks, but thankfully, the day of the ultrasound finally came. I'll never forget the tears that fell and continued to fall after I found out I was having a boy. "Can you check again?" I kept asking my doctor.

I didn't speak to my husband for days. I have to admit as foolish as it sounds now, I didn't even want the baby. I know people were annoyed with me. How ridiculous this was when so many women couldn't even get pregnant and would do anything to have my little boy. I didn't care; I was enveloped in my own pity party.

You see, I'd always been a planner. Everything was planned to a T, from my schedule to my life; I knew exactly what would happen next. Thinking about it now, I'm pretty sure the lack of control is what bothered me more than not having the little girl I'd dreamed of.

When I went into labor, I hardly knew it. A few pains and Nick was here. It was as though my small, thin body was made just for *this*–for having babies. When my eyes locked on Nick's, I knew. I loved him more than life itself, and the thought of not having him nearly suffocated me right then and there.

How stupid I'd been! How selfish! And I realized it more and more with each day that passed as we continue to create

Chapter 1: Stories That Inspire

memories together and as I watch him grow. Now, I couldn't imagine having a little girl. What on earth would I do with her?

Must. Have. Wine.

# Reason #10 • I fight the battle every day to not give my child the same body image issues I've lived with my entire life.

## Body Image

I'll never forget the day my daughter walked into my bathroom, turned around to show me her behind and asked, "Do these jeans make my butt look fat?"

I'm sure my jaw hit the floor. She was only four years old, and hearing her say those words broke my heart. I knew where the question had come from, and I vowed that moment to do everything in my power to change her thinking.

What is *body image*? Wikipedia says: "Body image refers to a person's perception of the aesthetics and sexual attractiveness of their own body." I say it's much deeper than that. We blame the media for today's assumption of beauty. Back in the day, we had Marilyn Monroe and more recently, Tyra Banks, who've been replaced by much skinnier versions of beauty such as Kate Moss and Giselle Bundchen.

So, the question I've asked myself time and time again: how do we get so screwed up? Is it society? Or the media? Or is it much simpler than that? I think my childhood explains so much of what I now call my "issues." I've been told I'm an attractive person, and I believe I am. Many of my physical attributes are desirable. Big lips. Large, distinctive green eyes. A smile that rarely goes unnoticed. All that and a figure that would've been applauded back in those Marilyn Monroe days. Yet, I grew up on diets…on different fads and physique-

# Chapter 1: Stories That Inspire

changing mentalities that have only further warped my already tarnished sense of self.

I remember in seventh grade my skin started to break out. Unfortunately, due to some not-so-great-genes, this trend continued beyond my period-starting and boob-growing days. My mom immediately put me on birth control to rein in both the insane breakouts and the out-of-control periods I was encountering. Immediately, I went from an average seventh-grade body to a grown up, much-bustier and more well-rounded body.

My mother had faced criticism from her mother all her life. So naturally, my mother also wanted me to be perfect. She explained that hair was 80% of your looks, so I focused much time on curling or fussing with my hair, trying to get the most beautiful style. She stressed the importance of makeup, so I never went a day without mascara and cover-up. I'll never forget the day she said, "Honey, your butt is looking big." And to be honest, it was. The birth control pills had kicked my hormones into over-drive, and my butt wasn't the only thing growing. In seventh grade, I went on my first diet. The cabbage soup diet was a big hit at the time, and my mother and I took it on like everyone else we knew. From then on, I began my yo-yo with weight-control, and the love-hate relationship I had with my body. The more I lost, the more control I had. And I sure *loved* control.

Some months I starved myself and when low-carb came out, it was a dream-come-true for the diet-addict! I watched my weight deteriorate along with my health, then bounce back up when I started eating normal again.

The main problem I have is wondering, honestly, would I have ever been overweight in the first place? I mean, yes, maybe I gained a few pounds due to the circumstances, but would I have actually ever been fat? Was there ever a true

Must. Have. Wine.

need to start dieting?  Was there a need for my mother to point out every time she saw a few extra pounds on my figure?  Did her constant criticism have more to do with my insecurities than anything else?

After years and years of working on myself, when I look in the mirror now, I see a strong, beautiful, curvy woman…most days. I still feel the pull from those *other* days when I want to pinch my fat roll, throw away the bread and swear off carbs. It's okay that I'm messed up. I mean, I can handle *that*. I can control it.

What I can't handle is thinking that my four-year-old little girl is going to have the same twisted thinking and lack of self-confidence I've battled my whole life.  I've watched my friends who have older girls make comments about their figures, and then catch their daughters also silently scrutinizing themselves in the mirror.  It's a domino effect we need to stop before it starts.  Our girls look up to us as if we are the smartest and most brilliant people on earth. We need to reflect in ourselves the people we want them to become.

Ever since that day in the bathroom, I've made a promise to myself that I would shut my mouth when I want to say negative things about my body. I now urge my daughter to be happy with herself, no matter how she looks or what she weighs. I'm trying to inspire her to love her uniqueness and focus on her strengths, not so much what *America* considers her flaws.  I tell her every day how beautiful and smart she is, and she *is*.  I'm not apologetic when I change my clothes or get naked in front of her, no matter how much I feel the weight of the change from bearing two children.  I pretend to love my body and all it has encountered.  I'm determined to teach her to ignore the world and what it's portraying as hot…and to create her own version of beauty…and rock it!

Chapter 1: Stories That Inspire

# Reason #11 • I should've trusted my gut.

## A Mother's Instinct

I was bawling my eyes out, even shaking a little. Okay, a lot; I was furious! My son was just about a month old and never had been the best eater. It was close to midnight and my husband stated that we needed to let him cry it out. I know we'd been reading that phrase in many of our books lately, but I thought it was too soon. *He's just too young.* But I was a new mom having a hard time deciphering between my instincts and what could be good advice.

With advice coming from everyone for everything, including my husband, I felt like I was losing my mind. In that moment, I thought maybe my husband could be right. Even though Luke had just had a full breastfeeding session, who's to say how much he really ate? He'd probably fallen asleep half-way through, and I hadn't been paying attention.

Truthfully, I was happy to be snuggling with him and watching *American Idol*. I wasn't noticing his every swallow. Maybe he's going through a growth spurt?

I couldn't take it! I'd probably let that poor little boy cry for 30 minutes before I broke down and ran in to grab him, crying and feeling so horrible that I could let him suffer like this. I immediately offered him milk. He ate furiously!! Was he starving? He was, wasn't he? I'm the worst mom ever!

That's now a night that even my husband realized we made the wrong call. We know it was just too early, *way* too early, to let him cry it out. I've now learned to trust my motherly

Must. Have. Wine.

instincts above books and advice…especially from rookie dads!

# Reason #12 • I'm going to have to let my baby go…one day.

## A Mommy's School Bus Jitters

I have no idea what it's actually going to be like watching my son get on the bus to head to Kindergarten for the first time, but I do know it's not going to be easy if I'm crying about it now and he's only 21 months old.

We read a few books every night at bedtime, and lately, our favorite book has been "Best Baby Ever" by David Milgrim. In it, the parents are mesmerized as their baby grows from his first smile until ultimately, they watch him get on the school bus for the very first time with tears in their eyes. I've read this book probably every night, at least once, for the last couple of months. Yet, tonight, I couldn't hold the tears back. It seems like just yesterday when I had my little 7 lb, 7 oz newborn baby boy. He's already grown so fast and if time continues to fly like this, I'll soon be watching a five-year-old get on the bus.

I start to choke up as I continue to read this particular night but I toughen up and tell the story until the end without him noticing my voice shaking. I conclude as I wipe the tears from my face that Kindergarten is a long way off, and I'm going to enjoy every single minute with my baby until then.

Must. Have. Wine.

# Reason #13 • I've had to learn the hard way that assuming anything regarding motherhood will backfire!

## Don't Ever ASS-U-ME as a Mommy

It's funny, thinking back on the misconceptions I'd had about parenting prior to giving birth to my daughter, Callie. I'd had several ideas in my head about how my life as a parent would go, and actually, many of which were wrong. By the time I had my son, Clayton, I had it all figured out. Don't judge, don't assume (we all know what happens when you ass-u-me) and definitely don't think you are going to be perfect. Seriously, you'll be eating your words.

My kids were never going to eat too much sugar. They were never going to watch **SpongeBob**. They would be in bed by 8:00 p.m. every night and they darn sure wouldn't be sleeping in any bed but their own! By the time they were one, they'd be off the bottle, and if they had a pacifier, guess what? That would be gone, too. My kids would never be the ones throwing food at the fancy restaurant, or talking back, or being a brat in public. We'd spend evenings similar to **The Brady Bunch** or the Cleavers, eating dinner together and chatting about our day, followed up by a puzzle or some other family-fun, learning-type activity. Ha! How ignorant I was!

Here's a little something I've learned as a mom of two children. When you want to pass judgment on other parents for anything…and I mean *anything at all*, think twice. And if you think you're going to do anything smarter or better when it comes to child-rearing, *think again*.

## Chapter 1: Stories That Inspire

I quickly found that it was my kids (both of them) throwing food at the restaurant, or talking back in front of company. I eventually gave in and let them go to bed super late *after* watching the dreaded **SpongeBob.** Both my kids have slept in our bed off and on, and I'm just thankful to be able to use the word "functional" when I describe my family. We are who we are, and we are far from flawless.

I love the mother I've become, and I love the children I've made, taught and love. However, I know I was just like all the other moms out there; I wanted to be perfect and I wanted to be the best. I judged others, thinking I'd do better. This race of motherhood isn't a competition of who can finish first with the fastest time on the clock; it's a silent war we must conquer in order to come out whole and sane when we cross that finish line. It's just *getting* there that's the true victory.

Must. Have. Wine.

# Reason #14 • I'm scared I'm not living up the promises I've made to my children.

### Please Promise To

Mothers make a simple promise to their newborn–to love them and care for them, no matter what it takes. It doesn't take long, however, for more complicated hopes and dreams to take focus in our minds. With unexpected economic heartbreak, career detours, and every day challenges that life is sure to deliver—and does, some of the promises we make to our children may feel like illusions. I learned this myself after becoming a stay-at-home mom. I went from having a successful career and being able to pretty much buy anything I wanted…to having to penny pinch and cut coupons. It wasn't like we were poor…but for the first time in a long time, I had to pay attention to my spending.

I soon realized that with our smaller income, new Gap and Gymboree outfits wouldn't be filling up my boys' closets. We wouldn't be living in an upscale neighborhood with the huge homes and white picket fences. I wouldn't be having gigantic, ridiculous birthday parties that my kids likely wouldn't remember anyway because they were too young.

I now see that it's through our disappointments we must realize that if we're providing our kids with the essentials of love and security, they will survive. More than likely, if we are the type of mothers that even have these worries, these children will *thrive*. Isn't it true that what we're already providing them is all they really need?

Chapter 1: Stories That Inspire

**Newborn**
Mother - I promise to give you all the love and care you will ever need and more.
*Child – Please promise to do exactly that.*

**Age 2**
Mother - I promise you'll have a great big grassy fenced-in yard to play in.
*Child – Please promise to spend quality time with me, whether it's inside our home or outside at the park.*

**Age 3**
Mother - I promise I'll give you a little sister or brother.
*Child – Please promise to provide me opportunities to socialize with other children my age and not just sit me in front of the television all day.*

**Age 5**
Mother - I promise you I'll send you to the best schools.
*Child – Please promise to spend one-on-one time with me after school, helping me with my homework and teaching me all that you know.*

**Age 10**
Mother - I promise I'll take you to Disney World.
*Child – Please promise to really listen to me, support my interests and let me explore my independence.*

**Age 13**
Mother - I promise I'll buy you all the right clothes.
*Child – Please promise to teach me to be confident in myself, no matter what I'm wearing.*

**Age 16**
Mother - I promise I'll buy you a car.
*Child – Please promise to teach me how to save money and earn the things that I want to have.*

Must. Have. Wine.

**Age 18**
Mother - I promise I'll send you to the University of your choosing.
*Child – Please promise to carve a path for me to do well in school so I may earn scholarships to get me through college.*

  We can get so hung up on giving them all the bells and whistles—the best schools, mind-blowing vacations and the trendiest clothes, but what really matters are the simple times you spend with them and enjoying each moment in our *today*.

CRISP & REFRESHING
*Riesling*
will complement this collection of stories that
amuse

# chapter 2

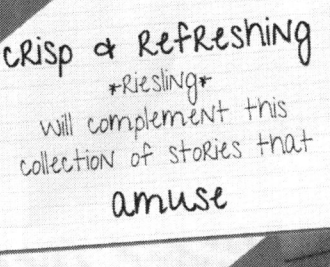

No better way to end a long day than to laugh out loud. These refreshing stories will have you chuckling as you reminisce of the same type of funnies from your own zany life with young kids. From the crisp anecdote to the darndest things those kids say; a glass of zesty Riesling is just what the doctor

follow!!

@musthavewine

# Reason #15 • I couldn't save my son from that evil McDonald's slide.

## I'm Not Lovin' It!

*I'm lovin' it!* Isn't that their slogan? On this hot spring afternoon in South Carolina, I was, in fact, *not* loving it. Actually, I wasn't minding it until my two-year-old son got stuck in the steamy, twisty, yellow and red slide at McDonald's. Up until that point, he'd been allowed to play at the Chick-Fil-A playland, but that slide wasn't nearly as loopy, as high up, or outside.

It never occurred to me that trouble could befall a child in such a wonderland. As I'm chatting with my folks, I hear what sounds like Carol Ann from *Poltergeist* summoning me from the TV. *Help me. Mommy, where are you? I'm afraid of the light, mommy.* I realize it is my little boy, somewhere at the top of the maze.

I can't see him, though I shout out to him. "Mommy's right here, baby, just slide down! I'm right here." I hear the fear in his voice and I start to panic. I tell my parents to stand by the slide to catch him, should he slide down.

I was going in! It's just a slide. Or is it? Is it a fire pit of tight twists and turns that drives claustrophobia into any adult who dares enter this little kiddie world? I'm pretty petite, and I often think I'm still 16…or at least in my 16-year-old body at age 34. *I'm not!* I slither up two turns and the heat is enveloping me. All I can hear are the echoing cries of my

Must. Have. Wine.

first-born. *I* want to cry. I can't breathe. I can't go up further. Someone help *me*! I may have a panic attack. I think of those moms who fight off intruders, who jump in front of a train, who hold their bare hands to their child's gushing wounds just to save their baby. And I can't climb the f*ck up a McDonald's slide? What's *wrong* with me? Disappointed in myself and scared for my son, I wiggle out of the entrance of the *fun* zone. Defeated.

I look at my parents; has he not come down? I don't know what to do. My heart is racing. Should I grab an employee, clearly trained like a medic, to scale the mountainous slide to save my son? Should I try again and climb through the kiddie tunnels of hell? All I could think about was my son's fear. Could he even see us? Did he think he was trapped for life? That he'd never again see his loving mommy and daddy? Before the tears start to gush out, the sweetest little seven-year-old girl comes down the slide, almost skillfully pulling my son by his ankle behind her. I run to him, grab him like he'd just been saved from a well like Baby Jessica.

I hug him so tight. He's crying. I'm crying. "Mommy is always right here, baby. Always!"

Once the emotions settle and we're safe in our car, I explain to him that he has to be brave in situations like that and slide down or climb back down (hmmm, nice advice coming from the mom who couldn't hack it herself).

Chapter 2: Stories That Amuse

# Reason #16 • Did she just ask about his penis? OMG, she did!

### Why Do Boys Have Tails?

Rylie was two years old when her cousins, Clayton and Callie, came to visit from Colorado. They'd moved when she was a baby so she hadn't gotten to spend a lot of time with them, and we were all excited. We all met up at Grannie Janet's house for a day full of fun in the sun with their new kiddy pool.

Clayton didn't have a swimsuit so his mom, Trina, just stripped him down naked and set him in the pool to swim. Rylie kept studying him and I assumed she was just checking the new cousin out. He was now over a year old, walking around everywhere and making noises as he tried to talk.

Rylie walked over to Trina and asked boldly, "Trina, why does he have a tail?"

Trina looked at her, confused, and asked what she meant.

Rylie pointed directly at Clayton's privates and said louder, "Why does he have a tail!?"

Trina burst out laughing and looked at me in delight before answering my daughter. "Why don't you go ask your dad?"

Must. Have. Wine.

# Reason #17 • How am I supposed to know everything?

## Giving My Kids the Sun, the Moon and the Stars

A couple of days ago as I drove the kids to school, Kate said from the back seat, "The moon is the sun."

I responded back to her in the manner I often do when my mind is on other things, with a dismissive, "Mmm hmm, yes."

Then I thought back to an article Mike had read about how children develop and thrive. The author's point was that children whose parents continue to challenge them in the absence of school (spring break, summers, etc.) and take advantage of educational opportunities wherever they exist, become more successful than children with parents like me. The author didn't mention me by name, of course, but I'm pretty sure it was implied.

So, when I thought of that article, I decided that Kate deserved a better response and further, a better life, than what I was giving her.

"Actually, Kate," I said. "The moon is a moon and the sun is a star."

"What, Mama? What is a moon?"

*Dang. I don't really know what a moon is.*
"The moon is a moon, kind of like a planet, but the sun is a big, bright star."

"The sun is a star?"

# Chapter 2: Stories That Amuse

*Oh, Lord, here it comes. She's going to ask me what a planet is versus a star. How the hell am I going to explain that to a four-year-old when I don't really know the answer as a 37-year-old?*

"Well, yes, honey, it's our brightest star," I began, now second-guessing if the sun actually was star. "It's kind of a nebulous body that gives us our light and our heat."

*Oh, great. Like she's going to know what nebulous means. Do I know what nebulous means?*

I started to kind of panic. Every time I tried to explain it in a new way, I used words or metaphors that I worried would elicit more questions from her. I wanted to feed her thirst for knowledge, but I wanted out of the current conversation because I knew I had no hope of explaining the intricacies of the universe to her. I should've stopped, but I blundered on. "You see, God created the earth and there was this big BANG..." *Okay, now I'm teaching creation* and *evolution in one breath–and neither one very well.* "There are nine planets (*there are nine, right?*) in our solar system." *What the hell does a four-year-old know about the damn solar system? What am I doing?!!* "We live on the planet earth and we have a moon that we call…the moon." *I am an idiot.* "The planets all revolve around the sun and it keeps us warm."

*What if she asks me what the moon does? I don't know what the moon does.* "We've sent people up all the way to the moon before. There's an American flag (and a Tri-Delta pin so the story goes) up there." *Why is my mouth still moving?* At this point, I could feel perspiration forming on my forehead. It was becoming ever clear that I was too dumb to have had children. At least I *knew* I was too dumb. Most dumb people don't know they're dumb. So, I guess I had one up on *them*. I began thinking about how much worse this would get when the girls would bring their homework home and ask me for help. They'd end up in remedial classes if I

Must. Have. Wine.

was the one to offer assistance. Mike was going to have to be their tutor.

I pictured the four of us sitting around the table in a few years. Mike would be explaining math or geography or something. Kate and Meg would have their books open and be listening intently. Then, pan over, and there's me. Furiously taking notes so as not to miss a word he was saying.

"Does any of that make sense, sweetie?" I asked Kate.

Silence.

"Kate?"

Silence.

I looked in the rear view mirror and there sat Kate, earphones on, staring at the TV screen. Watching **Mickey Mouse Clubhouse**.

Chapter 2: Stories That Amuse

# Reason #18 • Yes, they really *are* paying attention!

## 100 Bottles of Wine

My four-year-old, Audrey, always thinks it's hilarious to try and divert my attention, usually using an elephant or some other exotic animal, so she can tickle me on the neck. The other day I was cooking and she piped up, "Mom, look! There's a big white elephant outside!" prompting me to look out the window.

"An elephant isn't going to work this time." I told her, going about my cooking routine.

"Look, Mom! One hundred bottles of wine!"

I looked!

Then I laughed. Smart cookie!

Must. Have. Wine.

# Reason #19 • Sometimes you just have to work with what you've got!

## Bust a Move

Admit it! You know you've done some crazy things to either get your little one to sleep, to laugh or simply be entertained while you're waiting for the check to come after a surprisingly well-behaved dinner at Outback. If you're a mom and in your thirties, you may remember hanging out with some friends in their kitschy apartment after happy hour back in the 90s and watching that episode of **Friends**—you know, the one where Ross started singing *Baby Got Back* to his infant, Emma, trying to induce her second laugh. Later in that episode, an initially outraged Rachel—upset that she'd missed her daughter's first laugh, belts out the lyrics and throws in a little upper-middle class white-girl dance.

I've never been one to remember lyrics to songs; even the simplest nursery rhyme wouldn't come to mind when my first was born. I had *Twinkle, Twinkle* and *You Are My Sunshine* down, but I needed more. I'd try and sing my favorite Madonna or Jekyll & Hyde songs, and even after singing these for years and years, I could only remember a verse or two. Honestly, *Like a Virgin* wouldn't quite cut it anyway…

While rocking my four-week-old to sleep, one of my college sorority songs surprisingly belted out my mouth. Excited that I could remember at least one song, I sang it over and over. It wasn't the song where we shout out about our hotness, but a mellow song about loyalty. As my son finally shut his eyes, I'd transformed the song, replacing a few words to make it pertain to me and my baby. For over a year, it became part of

## Chapter 2: Stories That Amuse

our nightly playlist of Mommy songs. Did I mention we had a voice coach visit my college and that she point-blank told me to lip sync the songs because my voice wasn't working for her? I admit, I already knew. But it stung, anyway!

Regardless, my son acts like he enjoys my voice. When he started talking well, he'd ask for "One more song, Mommy!" Take *that,* voice coach!

One day recently we were watching **Diego** and the character announced they were on a hunt for an Anaconda. Direct out of that episode of **Friends**, I was sent right into Sir Mix-A-Lot's verse, *"Anaconda don't want none unless you've got buns, hun."* I enjoyed every minute of that, even though my son looked at me like I was nuts. And as kids do, he continually asks to repeat that episode and I've even got him rapping that line whenever they mention the snake.

I was relieved to hear a friend of mine had the same dilemma when her daughter was a baby. She was always struggling to remember lyrics to songs. One night in particular, after over an hour of trying to get her little one to sleep, while pacing in the hallway, she started singing "Humpty Dumpty"…not the Humpty Dance, but the nursery rhyme. Sure, maybe not a lullaby, but she used what she had. It worked, and sent her daughter off to dreamland.

Whether it happens to be a monologue from **Wedding Crashers** or the theme song to **America's Next Top Model**-*"Wanna be on Top?"*– if it works, don't be afraid to use what you've got.

## Reason #20 • Oops! Guess I better watch what I say!

### Choice Words

One day while cleaning the kitchen with my son playing nearby in the living room, I dropped a glass, and holding my breath, waited for the shatter. It just bounced. I breathed a loud sigh of relief.

That is, until my four-year-old quipped, "Mommy, aren't you going to say *oh, shit*?"

Chapter 2: Stories That Amuse

# Reason #21 • Well, now that I'm totally embarrassed once again…

## Watch What You Say

I was always telling Frank to watch the words he used around the kids. One day when Nathan was about three, Frank was going off about a man who owed him money. "I can't believe he did that to me. After all these years that piece of %&$* has really done it this time."

Nathan, who always looked up to his father, listened in admiration. I glared at my husband. "Frank, how many times do I have to tell you? Watch what you say around the kids!"

A few moments later, we heard a knock at the door. I ran to get it, Nathan trailing close behind. I opened the door, and maybe *not* so ironically, there stood the same man we'd just been talking about. I looked down and saw by the look on his face that Nathan had made the same connection—the light bulb had turned on.

"Daddy! It's the %$#* at the door!" he hollered over his shoulder, and then looked at me, a proud look on his face. "My daddy said you are a piece of %$@* and you better pay him the money you owe him."

As I ushered Nathan away from the door and the man he'd just unknowingly attacked, I passed Frank—who'd gone completely red with embarrassment. I couldn't help the smile that crept to my lips. After all, I'd told him–*watch what you say around the kids*! Maybe now, he'd listen.

Must. Have. Wine.

# Reason #22 • Everyone at church just heard him say the F word…everyone!

### Fire F*ck

One of the most hilarious memories of Alex as a toddler was his inability to pronounce the word "truck." For six months, it'd come out of his little mouth sounding like the "F" word.

One Sunday, we were visiting my parents in Murfreesboro, Tennessee and attending my very small hometown church. It was great to reunite with so many people I'd known practically my entire life. Of course, I was delighted to show off my son and tell them all about how he was growing.

It was time for the service to begin; everyone had just taken their seats and a hush settled over the congregation. At that very moment, a siren howled past the church and Alex announced loud and proud, "Mommy, I hear a *fire fuck*!"

I thanked God that the entire congregation just burst out laughing.

Chapter 2: Stories That Amuse

# Reason #23 • Pee, poop and spitup - all at once. Good times!

## A Newbie Mess

We were all sitting around the living room admiring our newborn son, Caleb. My husband's parents and sister were sharing the joy as we passed our swaddled love around the room. As new parents just home from the hospital, we were eager for all of these wonderful moments as a family.

Across the room, I heard Grandpa gasp, followed by a "*Whew!*" He was holding his nose and looking at me and my husband, and said, "Looky, looky! I think he made a poo poo!" Then he looked down at Caleb. "It's a stinky poo poo, isn't it?"

Up for the challenge, I laid Caleb on the couch while Kevin, on cue, grabbed the wipes and got in position. Ever so perfectly, I peeled the tabs of the diaper back and slowly removed it. Just a little poop, nothing crazy. Kevin wiped him. Holding Caleb's legs, I placed the diaper below his bottom. I bumped the diaper with my knee and it floated to the floor. So I grabbed his legs again as Kevin went for the diaper. Suddenly, a spew of black dredged down his leg onto our new couch and the floor. I couldn't do anything; I was holding the poor little guy's legs in the air. Kevin panicked and cupped both hands under Caleb's bottom, catching what he could in an effort to save our couch.

We screamed for someone to grab a new diaper, or a towel, or *something*! As I heard them shuffling, a spray of yellow shot out of Caleb. No catching that! And just as Caleb's auntie handed us a towel, my little boy turned, looked up at me as if

Must. Have. Wine.

testing our dexterity as parents—and spit up all over himself, and all over the clean part of the couch. Needless to say, my in-laws were in tears because they were laughing so hard watching the newbie parents in action.

# Chapter 2: Stories That Amuse

# Reason #24 • I dreamed of raising a soccer or basketball star...yeah, not so much.

## A Princess, Poop and the Game of Soccer

I'm so *that* mom at soccer games. I'm the one yelling for Callie to get the ball, cheering like one of those crazed women we used to hate at all of our own sporting events. Yep, that's me!

So, you can also imagine my disappointment when my four-year-old showed zero interest at her first practice. Oh, wait...she showed interest alright—it just wasn't in the ball. It was in the boys, the net...the sky, I mean—anything but soccer.

Rather than have a complete meltdown, I went to a woman I work with that has an amazing relationship with her daughter. She, of course, told me the obvious, "She's only four, Trina, and she's not supposed to be interested yet. She's only out there to have fun. Please don't turn out to be one of *those* moms!" I didn't tell her...*too late*!

So at the next practices and games, I watched the parents next to me closely. When they cheered or gave out pointers, I saw an appropriate opening and chimed in, too. I even ignored Callie adjusting her pretty pink bow and practicing dance moves on the field. I was so proud of myself. A future sport's momma in the works!

The following Wednesday, it was time for practice again right before our big Friday night game. We had pictures that day, so I had Callie's hair all fixed in cute little pigtails. As

Must. Have. Wine.

soon as we walked on the field, I saw a problem. Goose poop everywhere! And my little princess does not like to step in poop! I looked around, trying to figure out a game-plan, but none coming to mind. It was everywhere. It only took moments for her to notice. "Mommy, there's dog poop everywhere! I don't want to play!"

I reassured her we just had to get through pictures and then we'd see where we were. My little girl would barely bend down on the field to join her team for a group photo. I'm also pretty sure the photos will come back with her nose all scrunched up and a nasty look on her face.

Once photos were done, I sighed in relief—now we just had to get through practice. Callie took one more look around the field. "Mommy, I don't feel good!" She said, grabbing her throat. Both of her coaches approached her, feeling her head and rubbing her back.

"I don't think she feels good; she feels pretty hot," One of them told me, bringing her over.

I grabbed her hand and started walking her to the car. "Callie, are you sure you don't feel good?"

"No, Mom, my throat hurts." She paused for a moment. "Do you think they'll have the dog poop cleaned up by the game?"

I smiled. I knew it! Playing hooky to avoid stomping around in poop. Only my four-year-old! I tried to explain that it was actually goose poop and then left it alone, hoping she'd forget by Friday.

Friday morning my little princess awoke in a terrible mood. She was moving slow, and was surely going to make me late.

## Chapter 2: Stories That Amuse

"Callie Jo, you need to speed it up. We have to hurry." I rushed both kids in the car and we were off. As I looked in my rearview mirror, I saw Callie's arms crossed across her chest and a defiant look on her face. "What's wrong, honey?"

"I'm just telling you right now, Momma, if they haven't cleaned up that dog poop I'm *not* playing!"

Must. Have. Wine.

# Reason #25 • Just experienced the most embarrassing moment at my pediatrician's office.

## Cheetos and Marshmallows

It was that time of year, and I was at the office for my four-year-old's well-baby visit. The questions were the same thing they'd always been and I was ready for them. The doctors always wanted to know how my kids were sleeping, eating, drinking and pooping.

"Make sure she's getting enough fiber and fruits and grains," Callie's new pediatrician told me in a serious voice, as though this was my first time.

I was almost too quick to respond. "Oh, you don't have to worry about that," I said proudly. "We eat a lean protein, whole grain and veggie with nearly every meal. My family eats extremely healthy."

It was something I could honestly brag about; even my husband complained about the consistent health-friendly dishes on the menu at our house.

"That's great news! I love to hear it. Callie, what is your favorite food?" The doctor pressed my daughter, an all-knowing smile on her face.

Without hesitating, Callie responded enthusiastically, "Cheetos and marshmallows!"

Chapter 2: Stories That Amuse

# Reason #26 • The things we get to hear come out of our children's mouths!

## Broken Bum

Nathan was always jumping off the couch. He was two years old and rowdy as could be, so no matter how many times I told him to stop jumping, he'd still take the plunge.

"Nathan, if you keep doing that, you're going to break your bum," I'd tell him, folding clothes and shaking my head. It wasn't the furniture I cared about; he could break every piece and I wouldn't give a darn. It was always my kids' safety that had me worried.

"Its okay, Mama, I won't break my bum-bum," he said, and jumped again.

When the phone rang, I ran to answer while giving him a look to remind him to be careful. When I heard a loud crash, I bolted back into the room. Nathan sat on the floor, a pained look on his face.

"Don't worry, Mama, it hurts, but I didn't break it," he said, holding his little butt and running off into the bathroom.

I continued to talk to my sister on the phone when he came running in a few moments later, no shorts or underwear on.

"*Mama, Mama! I broke it, I broke it!* Look, there's a crack!" He turned to show me his precious little hiney and the crack that ran down the middle.

Must. Have. Wine.

# Reason #27 • You can't make this stuff up!

## Basic Primal Instinct

We were all excited that day. My husband had been traveling for almost a week and the boys and I missed him terribly. Not just because I missed his jokes and his sweet smile; I missed his help with the boys! I missed his help around the house… and I missed movie night with the other mommies.

The boys had colored "welcome home" signs to hold at the airport. I had them dressed and looking as clean as boys can look. I also had taken some extra time with my hair and makeup to look a little less like a mom who's been chasing toddlers for 120 hours. I'd just bought a new outfit and was excited to put it on. Especially since I'd recently lost 10 pounds…now just 10 more to go to be pre-baby weight!

My two and a half-year-old was bouncing around on my bed, while my 17-month-old checked out my closet. I put on my skirt and took off my "I'm just running to Target" t-shirt, and then my bra.

"Those are your boobs, Mama," my son said matter-of-factly.

*Yes, son, they are*, I thought, grinning.

He studied my bosom as I fastened my strapless bra behind my back. Then, he said, "I want to lick them."

I don't think I'll ever have to wonder about men and their fascinations anymore…they are simply born with them.

Chapter 2: Stories That Amuse

# Reason #28 • There's a little competition in this mama!

## The Birth of a Competitive Mom

On this particularly sweltering Easter Sunday, my parents and I, along with my two toddlers ventured out to our first-ever Easter egg hunt. Jump castles, face painting and games galore were scattered across a great, green lawn behind a church right in town.

The jumpy house for toddlers had the fewest in line. It always seems awkward–you throw your little tyke into an enclosure of mesh so he can bounce into a mess of strange, random little kids. We smile at them from the outside, patiently watching them go up and down, side to side, even get a little trample or two. Before long, they're bored and they slide out.

My 15-month-old was too young to participate in the egg hunt, which I'd soon realize why—so he stayed with my parents in the shade of some pines. I found our designated spot and prepared for the hunt. As we lined up, a various mixture of moms and dads with one or more children, I realized we still had time to wait before the ribbon was cut.

Under the hot sun, 20 minutes ticked by, seemingly longer than it does while you're waiting for your kids to finally fall asleep at bedtime. How do you explain the time issue to an excitable toddler who can see hundreds of colorful eggs lying just in front of us? As we stood, beads of sweat formed on my brow. The adults readied, closing in tighter and tighter at the ribbon, waiting for the volunteers to cut it. I wanted my boy to get a lot of eggs. But I worried about the other

Must. Have. Wine.

parents. Did they have a plan? So…quickly I devised one. We will book it, *Ninja-Warrior* style, to the middle and I'd kick eggs to my boy who will swiftly scoop them into our basket. I told my two-year-old of our master plan.

  Finally, we saw a chopper nearing us. The draw to this particular egg hunt was the promise of a helicopter flying direct and low over our field of eggs. Sure enough, they followed through as promised. This moment elated me as I saw my son's eyes fill with wonder as his hair whispered a dance of excitement, the little bunny nose they'd hand-painted on his cheek now smudging down his smiling little face. We cheered as the helicopter dropped more colorful plastic eggs into the roped-off hunt zone that beckoned us to begin! As it flew off, I was suddenly aware of butterflies in my stomach. What was this feeling? I just wanted to make darned sure my happy little boy stayed this way and grabbed his worth in eggs.

  This was the moment, folks–the birth of my parental competitiveness. I'd seen it on TV with pageant moms and baseball dads. I didn't know I had it in me. But suddenly, with my legs poised for the race, I had one mission. GET. LOTS. OF. EGGS.  In my imagination, I held my son like an NFL running back with a football, heading for the end zone. I don't remember the ribbon coming down; I just remember blocking and ducking and kicking and scooping. With about 30 eggs in my basket, I felt triumph! We won! I cheered with my son who could've cared less if we'd gotten 10 eggs. I was proud. Oh, the glory!

> The moment you're about to quit is usually the moment before the miracle happens.
>
> Don't give up.

chapter 3

### challenging & deep
*pinot noir*
will complement this collection of stories that encourage

When emotions are worn thin and it's hard to see the light at the end of the tunnel; this elegant wine reminiscent of sweet red berries, plums, and cherries is sure to lift your mood. The most challenging times we endure as a mom are often the times we feel most alone. During these deep moments, it helps to know you really aren't alone. Grab a box of tissues, and if it gets too emotional, don't worry; you can always pour another glass.

Chapter 3: Stories That Encourage

# Reason #29 • As moms, we survive through our strength.

## Surviving SIDS

It was a wonderful day. My daughter and I had been shopping with a friend of mine before coming home to spend the evening making Christmas cookies. My little girl was the light of my life and I spent every minute with her. We'd been getting ready for Christmas; it was going to be our first family vacation to Arizona. Little did I know my life was about to change.

The next morning, December 9, 2004, I woke up about 4:00 a.m. and made a bottle. I went in to get my baby girl, who was usually crying and ready to eat. I heard nothing when I went over to her crib to pick her up. She lay there cold and lifeless. I screamed. My husband came in and panicked, I yelled, "She's dead!"

"No, no she's not!" He yelled back, as frantic as I was.

We called 911. The voice on the other end of the line walked us through CPR but it wasn't working. Finally, the ambulance got there. I rode with my baby to the hospital as my husband followed in the car. They asked about medical problems, health issues…etc. There were none. I'm not sure I breathed the entire ride, and although it felt like a lifetime, we finally arrived at the ER.

Must. Have. Wine.

A huge needle was put in her arm and the paddles were brought out to attempt to resuscitate her heart. I looked at her tiny body and wondered how it could take a shock like they were sure to give. The doctor came over before they started the process.

"Even if we save her, she'll most likely be brain dead, due to how long she has been gone," He said, pressing to see if this was truly what we wanted.

I looked at my husband before answering, "Leave her alone if she is gone—don't torture her little body anymore than it has already endured." Then I sat with my husband and bawled my eyes out.

We went home, lifeless. The police came and questioned us separately like we were criminals, just before taking some of her things. I wasn't sure if it was harder to grieve and process the horrendous nature of what had just happened or to deal with the police pressure after losing our precious first-born child.

When we were done answering their questions, we took our dogs and went into God's country in the mountains and just walked in the snow for an hour, not saying much, crying a bunch and asking why. Why would God take our baby? She hadn't even experienced the world yet. She only had a little longer to go until her first Christmas.

We got the autopsy report back and they said it was SIDS—no real scientific answer to the question of why. Then, as if the nightmare was never to end, the sheriff's office sent a counselor to come out three days later, and he told us that 90% of couples who lose a child end up divorced. I was broken. *You mean to tell me that I've just lost my daughter and now I'm going to lose the only person in my life who truly knows how I feel?* I later called the office and told them that while this statistic

# Chapter 3: Stories That Encourage

may be true, three days after someone loses a child is not the time to share this information. I hope they've since changed their policy.

Three months passed and I sat at home with nothing to do but miss my baby girl. My husband and I decided to try again. We tried and found out we were having a baby boy due December 15, 2005. To be sure I didn't go into labor on the anniversary of the day our daughter had passed, my doctor got the okay from our hospital to induce me so my baby boy would have his own special day. When we brought our son home, he ate and slept like a champ and was the perfect baby. That first year, I was a wreck; I didn't want him to sleep. But he grew and grew–our happy and healthy little boy.

When he was 19 months old, we had our second son. He was not an easy baby; he cried all the time until we finally put him in his own room to sleep. When he was 14 months old, we wanted to try one more time for a little girl, and we got pregnant again. This time, I was so anxious I went as far to buy a DNA test and I *hate* needles of any kind. I had my girlfriend prick my finger and I sent in the sample. It came back - girl!! Oh, I was so excited and we decided we were going to name her after her sister.

It was a super hot day in August and I was having contractions but they weren't too bad. My husband insisted I go to the hospital, but I didn't want to go and sit there for three hours for a stress test just to be sent home. But I went, and to my surprise, I was seven centimeters dilated. I called my husband to come to the hospital and my cousin went to our home to take care of the boys. The doctor beat my hubby to the hospital and wanted to break my water but I wanted him to wait. I was very nervous, maybe because I thought it was a girl and I didn't want to have another tragedy. I kept feeling that terrible feeling like something bad was going to

Must. Have. Wine.

happen. What if something happened to me, and my kids would be left without a mommy?

Before I knew it, I'd had my fourth baby. I kept hearing, *oh he's so cute* and *he has dimples*! "I take it there's a wiener," I said to my husband, smiling.

"Yes, honey, there is," the nurse replied.

I was still a happy momma; he was healthy and perfect.

My babies are not babies anymore; Six, almost five, and almost three. We have pictures of their sister in our home and they know about her. They sing happy birthday to her and make cupcakes and eat one or two to remember her on her birthday. Every year, on the day she passed, we put up our Christmas tree to honor her—it's our family tradition. I'm not afraid to talk about her, and I want to be able to take my experience to help other new parents know the simple little things to help prevent SIDS, and that while it was a tragedy in our lives, we survived it. People always tell me that I'm not over it, and my response to them is you never get over it—you simply learn to deal with it, and you can't judge until you've been in the same shoes.

I try hard to let my kids be kids and not be over-protective, even though I don't have the attitude that nothing is going to happen to me-*because it did*. I want my kids to be daring—not afraid, and try new things. I push to just let go and have fun. I don't want to waste time because we never know how much we have. Jordan taught me that; every day is a precious gift. It's not how much time we missed, but how much time we shared together.

Chapter 3: Stories That Encourage

# Reason #30 • After months of fighting, our baby is finally declared healthy and disease free.

## Conquering Leukemia

Every pregnancy is a miracle. Every birth is another miracle. Hearing a Children's Hematologist/Oncologist say that your baby has been healed of leukemia…unimaginable.

My pregnancy was great. Labor and delivery flawless. I delivered a perfectly healthy eight pound, seven ounce, 21-inch full term baby girl on December 20th, 2010. Around 8:00 p.m. her pediatrician came in for a routine check. After looking at Vivi for a few minutes she ordered a CBC blood test due to an unusual rash on her stomach. By 10:00 p.m. she let us know that Vivi would not be able to room in with us that night as they needed to be able to monitor her more closely. The blood tests had come back slightly "abnormal" so they were taking all precautions. That night I fought through the new mom haze to nurse every 2-3 hours while my husband held her in between feedings. The next morning brought a chasm to our perfect universe.

Vivi's pediatrician came in to tell us that Vivi's test had been looked at by various specialists and were still "abnormal." The next words out of her mouth—"Leukemia. Her blood tests look like Leukemia."

The oxygen disappeared from my lungs. My vision blurred. I waddled as fast as I could to my room and burst into gasping, uncontrolled sobs. I wanted to scream at someone, anyone. Nothing really prepares you to hear "Your two-day-

Must. Have. Wine.

old baby probably has leukemia, but more tests are needed." Nobody prepares you to hear that your perfect baby is somehow imperfect in a horrible, life-altering kind of way. My mind started spinning with the details of how, why, chemo?  Was I really considering chemo for my infant?  How do we navigate this landmine?

We packed up our two-day-old baby and headed three hours away to Children's Hospital in Denver on December 22$^{nd}$. They took an impossible amount of blood from her tiny arm. We waited.  There would be no test results until after the holiday.  We waited and prayed.  We called upon our church family to pray for the healing of our baby.  This team is not your run of the mill prayer team.  They can throw it down, and I believe in the week they did, God heard.

Dr. Smith called. He said that Vivi's case was rare.  He diagnosed her with Transient Leukemia.  He believed that with time, her abnormal blood cells would be replaced with healthy ones.  All we had to do was wait.  He also said that her condition was abnormal because typically children with this blood disorder also have Down's Syndrome. She did not. We waited. We tested every week and then every two weeks. Little by little, cell-by-cell she was healed.

At four months Vivi was declared healthy, cleared, leukemia-free.  We had our healthy baby and a miracle.

# Reason #31 • I never thought I'd recover from the loss…but that was before I saw all I was to gain.

## Leaving It in God's Hands

I knew that getting pregnant at the age of 33 had its risks. We all know as women that with each uptick after the age of 30, you are getting closer to the dreaded age of 35 – meaning a higher risk for birth defects according to doctors. When I saw those two little pink lines after months of trying, I was ecstatic. My husband and I celebrated and shared the news with everyone. I couldn't wait to have this baby, to start our new family.

I'll never forget the day I started bleeding, I was only about eight weeks along. *No, this can't be.* We'd tried so long, but sure enough, the doctor confirmed my worst fears after arriving at the hospital. I'd miscarried.

I'm not sure which was more difficult–the actual pain of losing my baby, or having to relive it every time we had to tell those close to us I'd miscarried. Eventually, the pain subsided, and while I was scared, I knew time wasn't on our side and we had to start trying again.

This time, it only took a couple of months, and when I saw the two pink lines…I didn't jump for joy. I knew we had a long road ahead, and to be excited at this point would only be premature. We waited the full three months before telling a soul, and only then did I allow myself a bit of enthusiasm.

I remember going in for my monthly check up; my doctor had informed me we'd be taking tests. After everything I'd been through already, I knew I wanted to test for Down's Syndrome. I wasn't sure how we'd address it if a test came back positive—I just knew I wanted to know. Soon after testing, the nurse called me; the test results had come back abnormal, showing a possibility of Down's. I hung up the phone and curled up into a fetal position. I didn't know if I could handle anything else…how could God do this to me? It wasn't fair. I'd lost my first baby, and now this child could possibly have Down's Syndrome?

After a ton of thinking and talking with my husband…soul searching combined with praying, we decided to do the amniocentesis, even with the risks and possibility that the test could be incorrect. How could we make a real decision off a test that wasn't even 100% accurate?

We went through with the test, and waiting for the results was the most excruciating thing I'd ever done.

My son is now five years old and healthy! While we decided to not pursue having any more children because of the risks associated, I couldn't be happier. I know I'll never understand losing my first child, nor will I understand having to go through the stress of wondering if my second child would be healthy…but I'm now forever blessed with a son who brings so much joy to my life and I've learned to leave the rest in God's hands.

Chapter 3: Stories That Encourage

# Reason #32 • We had to take our first trip to the ER.

## Conscious Sedation

"What is that exactly?" I asked the pretty, brown-haired nurse attempting to soothe my hysterical three-year-old.

"Conscious sedation is where we heavily sedate them, but they appear awake. They can't feel any pain, but their eyes wander and twitch." She looked at me, and as soon as she saw what was sure to be horror in my eyes, she quickly added, "It's much safer for children in this age group—it's better than putting them under completely."

I stared down at my poor little girl, who was in so much pain; I didn't care what they did as long as they fixed it.

We'd been in the emergency room for about an hour. Earlier in the evening, Callie had been doing her normal nightly routine after having her bath, which included brushing her teeth and combing her wet tendrils of messy brown hair. As soon as she stepped up on her miniature pink princess chair to be able to reach the sink, it folded up and gouged her between her legs as her little wet body slipped and fell.

I held my daughter as she squeezed her legs together—patting her back and assuring her between sobs that it was going to be okay. Callie is pretty tough, so deep down I knew it must be worse than it looked.

"Where does it hurt baby, you're going to have to let me look at it."

Must. Have. Wine.

When I saw blood down running down her legs, I tried to mask the terror in my face as I hugged her little trembling body closer to mine.

We headed directly to the ER. With Callie in their care, the nurses and doctors rushed around me in a frenzy; it was a small hospital in an even smaller town so this type of injury was probably not something they saw daily.

We agreed to the conscious sedation; I wasn't sure I had any other choice. And when she fought as they gave her the medicine by injection, my first tears fell. They agreed to let me stay with her and I did, clenching her little hand in mine. I watched as she departed, her eyes rolling back in her head and the drool leaking out of the corners of her mouth.

They examined her and determined she had an external laceration—which, compared to the alternatives, was something we should be relieved about. A few stitches and we'd be good to go!

The first stitch made my daughter, who appeared to be heavily dosed on heroine or some other type of drug, cry out in pain as tears sprouted from her little eyes. I glared at the nurse, who'd been nothing but great the entire time.

"It's just the pressure," she assured me, lightly rubbing my back. "She can feel the pressure."

With each stitch, Callie screamed for me, louder and louder. Her eyes kept twitching and she kept drooling, making me cry even harder. I was about to lose it when my husband had to leave the room—he couldn't handle it either.

The feeling of being completely out of control when your daughter is in such deep pain is one of the most terrible feelings in the world. When they finally finished stitching her

# Chapter 3: Stories That Encourage

up, it took about an hour for her to come back to. The first thing she said, or slurred, rather, pretty much summed it up. "Mommy, I don't want to be a robot anymore, please make it stop."

My heart broke as she thrashed around, trying to get control of her body. About two hours or so later, she was able to walk a little—with assistance, and talk normally. And within a day or two, it was as if the little accident had never happened.

That's the wonderful thing about children; they are resilient. More so than we even are as mothers. Now looking back, I realize that the entire situation was harder for me than it was for her. She can't even remember getting the stitches, or the effects of the medicine. However, the things that happened that night will be forever etched in this mother's brain.

Must. Have. Wine.

# Reason #33 • How do I explain death to my baby?

## A Pony Named Sage

Michelle had always been my little horse lover. From the time she could walk, she had a pony and was riding. Our whole family spent weekends with our horses. Every Saturday morning, we'd all get up early and get the animals saddled for a trail ride. Michelle, by four years old, was quite the little rider. She had no fear. I was a stay-at-home mom, so she also got to spend a lot of time during the week with her little pony, Sage. She woke up extra-early every day, went to the kitchen to get an apple, and ran outside to give Sage her morning snack before the rest of us were even awake. Sage was her pal.

One morning, I woke to a quiet house, which was unusual. Most mornings, I was awakened by Michelle shaking me, hollering for me to get up. Where was my little daughter this morning? I put on my robe and hurried out the door, realizing exactly where she was. It was barely dawn, but I knew I'd find her outside petting our sorrel pony. Sage was a wonderful little mare. Ponies had a bad reputation for being moody and mean, but not Sage. She was probably just too old to kick up a fuss; we never did find out her true age.

As I got closer to the fence line, panic fluttered in my stomach and rose up into my throat. No Michelle. No Sage either. *Where were they?* I scanned the pasture, trying to see if maybe Michelle had taken off after Sage, although that wasn't likely. It was as though Sage sensed her little four-year-old owner as soon as she walked on the front porch—she'd come galloping toward the fence line to greet her. With each year, it became more of a hobble really, but Michelle didn't notice. She loved that little pony and thought she was perfect.

Still, no Michelle. I finally found my voice and started screaming, *"Michelle Lynn, you better come back here now!"*

Out of the corner of my eye, I noticed a growing spot on the horizon and a little hand waving at me. I started running as I confirmed it was my toddler, riding her pony. As I crawled through our wooden fence, she approached with a huge smile on her face. It was only then that I noticed the orange twine wrapped around Sage's nose into a make-shift bridal, coming back into reins Michelle was maneuvering.

"Hi, Mom!" she yelled. Her grin was wider than I'd ever seen it. How on earth had my baby gotten up before me, made a bridal out of twine and gotten on her pony, riding off toward the sunrise all by herself? I was filled with pride, mingled with shock.

It was six months later when I found myself walking outside in the early morning, once again looking for Michelle. I had breakfast started and couldn't find her inside. As I approached the gate, I noticed her small figure, curled up over a large pile of something in the grass. A lump grew in my throat. I wanted to call out, but I couldn't. As soon as I heard Michelle's sobs, I knew. Sage had passed, waiting by the white wooden fence for her friend to come out like she did every morning. I felt a stream of emotions come over me. I didn't know how to react, so I just climbed through the fence and held my precious little girl, rocking her as the tears came down.

I felt more scared that day as a mother than I'd ever felt. I realized that I was going to have to explain death to my little innocent four-year-old. Pets were just the

Must. Have. Wine.

beginning...grandparents, friends...anyone. I realized suddenly that motherhood itself was much bigger than just me...and I was terrified. When she finally could talk through the sobs and ask me *why*, I gently told her, "Sage went to heaven honey, like we all do at some point. She will be waiting for you there."

Chapter 3: Stories That Encourage

# Reason #34 • I just dropped my baby off at daycare for the first time… and my heart is broken.

## A Valentine's Broken Heart

I had no doubt my heart would be broken that Valentine's Day in 2007. You see, I'd given birth to my baby girl on January 21$^{st}$. Just over three weeks had passed and I was standing on the doorstep of a woman I'd barely even spoken with, ready to hand over my precious newborn.

Holding back tears, I stood there for what seemed like eternity, staring at the door. It was a beige door, framed by a pretty, upscale brick house. I guess that should've made me feel better in some weird, only-in-today's-society kind of way. She had a nice house, so surely—she was a good person? That's the way it works, right?

I kept staring, holding my sleeping infant close to my chest. I'd dressed her special that day in cute little jeans with a heart on them and a matching heart onesie. Being a new mother, I didn't know the obvious…that jeans were uncomfortable and that babies actually preferred to be in soft clothing. Well, at least she was festively matched for the holiday on her first day of daycare.

I reached my hand up to knock, but then I heard Callie whimper and I quickly pulled away. I patted her soft head of dark, messy hair. Why was I dropping her off only after three weeks I again asked myself?  Oh yes…that's right. *I had to*. I'd been working in an insurance agency for about two years. I only had three weeks of time to take off, and with my

Must. Have. Wine.

husband and me struggling to make ends meet ...that's all I could take. Besides, I was lucky—wasn't I? Most of the other ladies in my office with children had taken only two weeks off.

Pulling me back into reality, Aurea, a petite, beautiful Puerto Rican woman opened the door. I wondered if I'd even knocked. Her eyes filled with confusion as she waved me inside. "Come on in, Trina. How long have you been out here?"

She seemed to sense my fears, or at least knew of them due to past experience, and gestured for me to sit on her couch. Her white carpet looked impeccable, not a spot anywhere. I looked around at the five other young children playing with toys, wondering how on earth she kept her house so perfect. Not a speck of dust anywhere on her expensive furniture. Was this a good sign?

I didn't think so.

We chatted for a few minutes, mostly me reminding Aurea of Callie's schedule. I laugh now at this notion—schedule? At three weeks? There was no schedule! And the gleam in Aurea's eyes said she knew this, too.

I hugged my tiny baby girl close to my chest, and then turned her over to someone else for the first time. Aurea immediately placed her in a bouncy chair and bustled off into the kitchen, which made me only want to stay longer. She should be held! *All the time!* Trying to stay strong, I forced myself to leave, and drove away, crying. And not just a tear or two...real tears. A veritable deluge washing down my face. What kind of terrible mother leaves her baby at such a young age? What kind of life was I already setting her up for? Little did I know, it was only the beginning of the long list of failures I'd blame myself for as a mother.

Chapter 3: Stories That Encourage

I did call to check on Callie about four times that day; thankfully, Aurea was patient and friendly. Although I was concerned about leaving my daughter, I knew deep down, she was in great hands. I'd specially picked Aurea, who had a huge list of references. Three or four ladies ran a daycare in the town where I worked. They worked together and were friends—all coming with high recommendations and all typically full and taking no more kids. I still think of Aurea as a huge blessing.

Sometimes, as mothers, we know what's best for our children…even if it's tough and tears us apart. I believe that Aurea brought something to, not only my child, but my family. She was patient, loving, smart, and incredibly experienced in the area of child-rearing and caretaking. By the time Callie was two, she was taking naps at the same time every day. She was cleaning up and putting all her toys back where they belonged. She was eating a well-balanced lunch and not complaining a lick about it. She was reading books and singing songs I never thought a two-year-old could sing. And she had a heart of gold and a giving nature that I believe only partly could've been born in her and partly taught to her.

*Must. Have. Wine.*

# Reason #35 • My child encouraged me to be brave.

## A Toddler's Insight

Your child can break your heart the way no one else can. They touch your emotions like you never had imagined before you had children. You love them like no one else you've ever loved, or even thought of loving.

My husband and I'd basically been fighting since my daughter was born. It was as though a competition had ensued–my husband and my four-year-old daughter against one another for my time. With Samantha, it was easy. She just wanted my time. She wanted to be held, read to, and fed…everything every little girl wants from her mommy. Rick, well…he wanted much more. He wanted my time, my mind, my body—everything I had to give, even at the end of the day when I had nothing left.

Most of my friends have children too, so I know how a normal family generally operates. They work as a team, the other parent stepping in when one needs help. They go on outings together, vacations…you name it. Not us. Rick sat in front of the TV, a beer in hand, watching the game every night. When Samantha would come over and ask him if he'd go outside to play with her, he'd crane his head around her to see the game, rather than listen to his own daughter. Even though she was used to it, I usually tried to make up for it by over-compensating my love and affection—it broke my heart.

How could the man I fell in love with turn out to be such a terrible father and husband? In our early days, he'd done everything for me. Opened doors, bought lavish gifts, and

# Chapter 3: Stories That Encourage

totally romanced me. Up until Samantha, things had been perfect. What had gone wrong? The books say that sometimes the man can become jealous of even his children's time with his wife. In other words, men can be selfish children. And the best way to deal with it is to try to divvy up your time and affection so everyone feels loved equally.

How in the hell could I divvy up more time? I was trying to be the mom, the wife, and also the breadwinner as I was working full-time. I looked at him with disgust, seeing his feet propped up on the coffee table as I slaved away in the kitchen, all the while helping Samantha draw at the kitchen table. How could I give myself to this man at night when he couldn't even give his family a second look during the day?

After one particularly loud and ugly fight, Rick stomped out of the house, slamming the door. It was after Samantha had gone to bed, and I was sure he'd woken her. I was sitting at the table with my head in my hands in defeat. How could I win this? I couldn't divorce him; he was Samantha's father and I didn't want her to grow up without him. But what kind of life were we offering her together? All he did was sit on his butt and take up space and make messes. He did offer financial support, which I had to have. As I wiped away the tears, I found some resolve. I'd stay in this marriage, even if it killed me. I had to do what I had to do for my beautiful little girl.

As I was about ready to go to bed, I heard little tiny feet crossing our wood floor. I looked up from the table and there was my little Samantha. Sure enough, the fight had awakened her.

I quickly wiped my eyes and tried to appear put-together. "What's up, buttercup?" I said, pulling her into a tight embrace.

Must. Have. Wine.

My four-year-old pushed me away and her big blue eyes looked into mine solemnly. "Mommy," she said. "I think you should get a divorce."

I'm still amazed at Samantha's insight into the entire situation at such a young age. And now looking back, I realize that she'd been just as much a part of the terrible life Rick and I had together. I'd been holding onto something for her all along, when all she wanted was for her and I to be happy. It breaks my heart that I put her through four years of misery, but I'm happy to say we've had ten long years of happiness since. And although I can't make those years better or take them back, I can make the future whatever I want it to be.

Chapter 3: Stories That Encourage

# Reason #36 • I survived three months of constant crying, I can survive anything!

## Colic - Every Mother's Worst Nightmare (At Least One of Them)

Three days prior to the birth of my second daughter, my mom died. Even after a few weeks had gone by, I was still trying to cope with the loss of my mother, while trying to console my six-year-old daughter who missed her grandma. At that time, my newborn daughter, Katrina, was diagnosed with colic. I was devastated. Basically, she screamed on and off from the time she woke up until she went to sleep. Being one who lacked patience already, I thought I'd surely lose my mind.

When my oldest daughter, Michelle, was four, she'd lost her dad to a terrible car accident. I'd raised her by myself for a year, struggling to make ends meet. When I met Nick, I knew I'd met the one for me. He was handsome, charming–and younger! We immediately hit it off and were serious within just a few months. He begged me to marry him, but I'd already been married. I didn't take the subject lightly. After about a year of dating-*surprise!*-I was pregnant. And nine months later, my princess, Katrina was born.

Katrina is a perfect example that we're able to handle more than we think we can. My first husband had died, then my mom had died, and now my newborn daughter was diagnosed with one of the most feared child-ailments, as it was such an unknown to doctors. Nick and I tried everything. We tried putting her in her car seat on the washer and dryer. We tried running the vacuum cleaner next to her, hoping the sounds and vibration would do the trick. We tried

Must. Have. Wine.

drops; we tried massaging her belly and back. We tried everything! We even tried driving her around right before bedtime. Nothing worked. All we could do was walk around, bouncing her, keeping her in motion and singing to her. That would eventually soothe her, and although she wouldn't sleep, she'd stop crying for small periods. We even had this Chinese restaurant we'd go to where the same server always waited on us. As soon as we got our food, she'd take Katrina and walk her around the restaurant so we could eat. Needless to say, it was the only time we went out, and she always got a huge tip.

For three months, this continued; the constant crying and wailing was almost more than I could bear. I thought I'd have to make an appointment with a doctor to give me something, *anything* to be able to deal with the stress. I was also planning my wedding; I'd finally agreed to tie the knot and make it official. The day we said our vows, a miracle happened. The crying stopped. I will never forget it. Katrina was three months to the day, and she smiled. She had never smiled, and she was smiling! My love for her grew bigger than even words can describe. Together we'd conquered these battles; these trials and tribulations that had begun even before she was born.

During that difficult time, those three months seemed like eternity. I never thought they'd be over. I never thought we'd recover from all the heartache. However, within almost a day from when she was better, I was better. The memory of the crying was already distant, nearly gone. As mothers, I believe we're programmed to sustain and survive…with only a flicker of the painful memories left for us to remember.

Chapter 3: Stories That Encourage

# Reason #37 • I don't want to go home to my crying newborn…

## This Too Shall Pass

It's every mother's worst nightmare, or at least—one of the many of our worst nightmares. I'd just left the doctor's office, sobbing. The dreaded diagnosis, the nemesis of all newborn mommies–colic. Callie was about three weeks old when she started the crying. Sure, like any other newborn, she cried some, like when she was hungry, or tired, or simply had a typical belly ache. But this was different. She began crying every night right around dinnertime, inconsolably. She didn't want to eat, she wouldn't sleep; there wasn't a single thing we could do that seemed to help.

Our lives pretty much got put on hold during that time. We couldn't accept dinner plans because we knew Callie would start bawling and it would ruin everyone's fun evening. We couldn't even really have a relaxing dinner together in our own home. I started getting something together the night before (God bless Hamburger Helper!) because I knew my husband or I'd be pacing a worn trail in our carpet, walking our little princess back and forth as we tried to calm her down.

Gas drops? Don't work. Driving around in the car? Didn't work for us. The dryer? Did that work for anyone? It sure didn't work for Callie. We found a recipe for onion water I'd heard worked wonders—but luckily for everyone that was *after* Callie was already better.

By week five, I'd about lost it altogether. I didn't even want to come home after work. What mother doesn't want to

Must. Have. Wine.

come home from work to see her brand new baby? I started feeling guilty, I started feeling resentful. I was crying daily. I felt like it was my turn to cry after listening to it for hours every night.

So, it was time. I called the doctor and made an appointment. As I walked into that tall café au lait building with people bustling out the doors and traffic horns blaring behind me on the street…I knew. I'd always known what the diagnosis would be. When I was a baby, I'd suffered from colic myself for three entire months. My poor mom dealt with this exact same thing for *three* months! Looking a lot like payback for me…

I had one of the best pediatricians in the valley. He was amazing, and so I never doubted his judgment. However, this particularly blistering hot summer day in Oklahoma, I was booked with his replacement as my doctor was out for the week. He asked me a total of about five questions, listened to her heart and looked in her ears, and then looked at me with sad eyes–as if he truly felt sorry for me because he knew he was going to deliver the worst news possible.

"Colic," he said softly. "She has colic."

Thank goodness for everyone there, I didn't start bawling…or punch his lights out for looking at me as though he actually understood how I was feeling. He couldn't possibly; he had no children…and he was a man.

"But," I stammered. "How on earth can you know? Isn't there a test you can take?"

He shook his head. "Colic is tricky. There are no tests and we aren't 100% sure we even truly know what it is. We do know it's an upset stomach, it usually lasts from about three

# Chapter 3: Stories That Encourage

weeks to three months of age, and the crying occurs around the same times every day—usually in the evenings."

I looked at him incredulously. "What can I do?"

He patted me on the back. "Be patient. Try the drops, although they only work for some babies." He spoke like he was wishing his golfing buddy good luck on the next hole, and then he left the room.

When the tears finally did come, they didn't stop for a long time.

Thank God for a friend who suggested Nutramigen formula. Sure, it was an arm and a leg for a tiny can that only lasted a few days…but it changed Callie dramatically for the better. Within three days, the crying had stopped and she was a new baby. The formula is for babies with a cow's milk protein allergy. Several other babies around Callie's age also diagnosed with colic tried the formula and had success.

The feeling of resentment towards that little being who has no control over the way she was feeling was heartbreaking. To not want to come home to see your new baby; to not feel utter love when you are pacing the hallways with her is devastating. You feel like you'll never get through it. But know that you can. You *will* get through it. Know that while you feel broken down now, you only feel stronger when it's over—more prepared to survive the next challenging steps of motherhood.

Must. Have. Wine.

# Reason #38 • I do realize how blessed I truly am.

## Just Breathe

Just after 9:03 a.m. yesterday, I stifled a sob as I watched NBC's coverage of the anniversary of the September 11th tragedy, my family bustling around me. At our cottage by the beach–our vacation timeshare–my mom and husband cooked breakfast. My dad sipped coffee on the balcony. My two sons raced circles around the kitchen island. I was engrossed in this telecast straight from Ground Zero.

It hit deep in my soul when a 12-year-old girl was telling her daddy that he was the best ever and will always be in her heart. This daddy left *her* world when she was just two. My boys are about that age. It was at that moment that I truly accepted what my husband had said to me just the night before.

"We need to be so grateful. We have one another. We have healthy children. We have our lives," he said when he came to bed, after he'd watched a 9/11 documentary. Half asleep, I agreed…mostly wanting to be grateful for lots of sleep.

I often feel like I can be swept up in the challenges of life and that it's hard to find things to be thankful for. But there's so much to thank God for; I am blessed with my family, friends and our health. But I always find a way to go back to…*if I could just make a little more money…or if we could just sell the house*…or whatever material wants I can think of at that moment.

# Chapter 3: Stories That Encourage

Yet, I see it now. *So what* if times are tough and the timing is off to sell our house. We get to watch the joy in our sons' faces as they float on top of wave after salty wave as we vacation by the sea. Sure, we wish we had a little extra cash so we could afford to redo our kitchen. But we *are* able to enjoy a few nice dinners out with the family this week. Yet again, another fantastic illustration of gratefulness bestowed...we are able to *be* with our kids, with *each other*.

We are lucky. We are blessed.

Through every tantrum, every cup of spilled Crystal Light on a clean floor, every exhausted 2:00 a.m. wake up call. Every single moment you wish you could have just a *little* space to breathe. Be so grateful for all you have. And breathe...because you *can*.

chapter 4

BE AS HAPPY AS POSSIBLE

fresh & sparkling
*moscato d'asti*
will complement this collection of stories that
**delight**

This fruity white wine is perfectly paired with the sparkling, fun and often funny moments in motherhood. Pour a tall glass, grab a sherpa blanket and prepare to enjoy this fresh collection of stories that may make you giggle...and will definitely make you smile.

Chapter 4: Stories That Delight

# Reason #39 • I'm pretty sure everyone has seen or touched my boobs now…

## There's No Such Thing as a Modest Mother

I'm sure someone warned me that upon the birth of your child, all modesty flies out the window. First of all, on the delivery table, they have you essentially naked—with a small gown and legs spread-eagled for all to see. Then they have nurses coming to look around in there, to poke and prod and supposedly diagnose progress. If I knew how many people would've been staring at my hoo-haw, I may never have had the guts to give birth!

So, at least you're warmed up when it comes to breastfeeding, right? Immediately after the doctor pulls this huge being (okay, maybe not so huge, but it sure feels like it!) out of my body, I don't even have a second to recoup before the nurses are grabbing my breasts, trying to get the perfect position for my young boy to feed. We spend the next hour of his life letting him suck, let go, and then latch back on. It's apparent that hardly anything is coming out and my poor son is getting frustrated, crying in between feedings.

The next few days aren't much better in the hospital. Every time a nurse comes in, she's plopping out one of my breasts like it's one of her medical tools, and pressing my son to me. She doesn't hesitate to stick her hands in there to help re-adjust as needed; we have to get the right position or I'll be sorry later, she keeps reminding me.

Must. Have. Wine.

My milk still hasn't come in, but when it does…that's enough to make someone want to lose it. My boobs inflate as big as balloons; my poor nipples are stretched beyond belief and leaking. I'm so sore, I just want to have a hot bath and forget about this entire ruckus. My son has a different agenda.

By the time I leave the hospital, I vow if anyone ever touches my boobs again, I may punch their lights out. But, within an hour, I'm sitting at home—doing…guess what? You got it—*breastfeeding*! I can't go anywhere because my precious angel has quite the appetite and is basically attached to my chest 24/7. Didn't somebody say this was supposed to be a time of bonding? If masquerading as an open-all-night 24-hour diner equals "bonding," I guess that's what's happening.

Within a few days of being home, my breasts are still sore; blisters surround my nipples. He's obviously been latching on wrong. That damn nurse was right! So off to the hospital I go for one more poor woman to grope my boobs and show me what I'm doing wrong.

It's amazing what mothers can endure…it truly is. Eventually, my son and I got the breast-feeding thing down. We'd feed at the same times pretty much so I was free to do things as needed in between. Hey, when the time called for it, nobody said feeding in the car, pulled over on the side of the road, was a bad thing. Desperate times call for desperate measures.

At three months, when I had to return to work, I decided to let the breastfeeding go and buy bottles and formula. Rather than be elated as I'd been expecting, I was depressed. I went back and forth on the decision probably a hundred times, driving both myself and my husband crazy. Deep down, I'd become attached to those moments alone, rocking and feeding my son. I was giving him something no one else could, and although those first few months were tough—I knew I didn't want to let it go.

## Reason #40 • Potty training success: check!

### It's All in the Aim

I was proud of my son who'd gotten the hang of potty training at 18 months. By 22 months, he was a pro! We were even leaving the house with his big boy undies on, taking the extra time to stop in the public bathrooms (or the secluded tree at the park) so he could go when he had to. Now he's two years old, and one day I couldn't believe what I was seeing when I turned the corner into the kitchen and saw my little boy standing there, naked from the waist-down, with slightly bent knees, precisely peeing into the Mega Blok toy he held out in front of him.

I laughed and told him he shouldn't do that, that we only pee in the potty…but secretly, I was proud. Until the next day, that is, when I caught him aiming for his beach pail he'd purposely placed on the floor. This time, I had to act stern and guide him to the potty.

Over the course of the next week, probably no thanks to my initial reaction, I caught him aiming for all sorts of toys with a look of pride on his face. Funny as it was to me the first couple of times, it was starting to grow old. I had a serious talk with him, as serious as a talk can be at 24 months, and in just a few days, he was focused on the potty again.

Almost three now, he still occasionally pulls down his pants and smiles…waiting for a reaction.

… Chapter 4: Stories That Delight

# Reason #41 • Our children are designed to be just who they are going to be… even at a very early age.

## A True Princess

My granddaughter, Iryna, was always a true princess. From an early age, she loved to get all made-up and wear poufy dresses and pretty shoes. I loved watching her; she was a dainty little thing in those days and she even walked like royalty. When other kids were playing in the mud, Iryna was walking around the puddles to avoid getting her pink waders dirty, not a hair out of place. Everything she did was with her best manners, always quiet and never loud or obnoxious. I adored that little girl with all of my heart.

One day, Iryna and I were having a deep conversation which wasn't unusual, even though she was only three years old.

"Grandma, are you getting old?" she said, a serious expression on her face.

"Yes, dear, I am getting *older*." I tried to keep it light, with a smile on my lips as I folded the stack of clothes I'd been working on all morning.

She tilted her head, her beautiful red hair spilling over her shoulder. "Well, Grandma, does that mean you will die?"

"Yes, my darling, I will someday pass away." I put the pair of trousers I had folded on the couch next to me and paused, waiting for her reaction. Death was a very delicate subject with such a young child; I hated to broach it too early. What

Must. Have. Wine.

if now she would always be thinking about when I would be gone?

Iryna sat silently for a few moments, an upset look on her face. "Grandma?" she said finally. "Who will wear all your dresses when you die?"

Chapter 4: Stories That Delight

# Reason #42 • Score! My son likes the ladies!

## Ladies' Man

My son has always shown the signs of being a man's man, even at the young age of two and a half. I remember making one of our daily trips to Target when he was just 10 months. As we passed the lingerie section, my son, eyes wide open, let out "oooohhhhh" and smiled a big toothy smile in that direction. Without fail, almost every trip after that, he'd react the same way. I didn't teach him this! He never goes into any store with his father, so he didn't get it from him. And he sure doesn't have this reaction passing the cars, trucks or bikes!

It didn't matter what store I was in, when we passed the ladies' intimates, he'd give out a little smirk of enthusiasm. Now at almost three, this fascination hasn't left him. We were browsing around Old Navy one day. He's always been a pretty good listener and can keep up with me as I stroll his brother around. I heard his footsteps stop behind me and I looked around but couldn't immediately see him.

"Kade," I called out. "Kade, you've got to stay where Mommy can see you. Where are you?"

"I'm here, Mommy."

I turned to follow his voice and found him standing at the foot of a pretty little girl mannequin, holding her shirt up and poking her belly button. I'm sure I flushed beet red, but couldn't help the smile that emerged. Ever since then, he gets a little giddy when we pass a cute mannequin and instead of

Must. Have. Wine.

"ohs," he now points out that "those are for boobs," referring to the intimates.

My boy, always making his daddy proud!

# Reason #43 • Boys will be boys!

## Full Tank

My four-year-old son, Gage, and I had gone out to eat with his Grannie and Grandpa. As usual, my rowdy little boy was excited and rearing to go. I kept reminding him we were in a public eating establishment and he had to be good.

It was crowded, so I was glad when he settled down a bit and started eating. Then, out of nowhere, a huge belch escaped that little mouth. The entire bustling restaurant stopped and stared.

I was mortified. "Gage Vance!" I hollered. "Say excuse me! That was very rude!"

Gage looked at me pointedly as he rubbed his belly. "Mama, it just means my tank's full!"

Must. Have. Wine.

# Reason #44 • I have created a high-maintenance four-year-old.

## Starbucks Anyone?

Callie Jo Epp. Where do I start? She was one special little girl from the day she was born. Our first-born child and one of the first granddaughters—she was pretty much spoiled from the get-go. I styled her in Gap and Old Navy–pretty pink dresses and fashionable matching shoes. How could I help it? Anyone who goes shopping for a baby girl can attest; they have the absolute cutest clothes available and it's downright addictive.

Another habit we started early was taking our daughter to Starbucks. You know you're in trouble when your baby girl can only say a few words, including "Mommy," "Daddy," and then "Starbucks!" as we drive by the familiar green sign. We were doomed!

Callie always knows exactly what she wants to order when we head to my all-time favorite coffee shop. Kids' hot chocolate, a vanilla or chocolate milk box, and usually a vanilla bean scone. Admittedly, my four-year-old happily walks up to the cashier and politely orders whatever her little heart may fancy that day.

One particular day we were in a huge hurry because I had to be at work in 35 minutes and had about a 25-minute commute, which included dropping my kids off at daycare. I'd run out of creamer that morning, and let's face it, folks, no coffee means zero brain power for this career woman. So, off to Starbucks we went with an excited toddler pondering what she'd order. When we got to the drive-thru, I sighed.

# Chapter 4: Stories That Delight

Three cars in line equaled me being very late to work, and oh, how I hated to be late! Callie couldn't have said it better. "Mommy, if these people don't hurry, we are never going to be able to get our coffee, right?"

Thinking about how late I might be, I said in a monotone, "Yes, honey."

"Mommy, maybe you should just crash them out of the way!"

I looked back and saw the serious look on Callie's face. She meant it!

"Honey, we can't crash into them. That's not reasonable! If we're just patient, they'll move soon."

Funny thing though—I'd also been thinking how nice it'd be to ram my car into the back of the person in front of me who evidently hadn't decided ahead of time what they'd order. Finally, it was our turn. Before I could tell the nice woman at the other end of the microphone what I wanted, Callie piped up as loud as she could, "*Come on, people, move it!*"

Must. Have. Wine.

# Reason #45 • Our family secret revealed!

## The Pee Tree

We had a Pee Tree at our home where my children grew up. My four children all used it, and my eight grandchildren still use it to this day. It began as sort of a joke when potty training. When we were outside playing, I'd bribe my boys throughout the day. "If you have to potty, you can just pull it out and pee by the tree!" It worked like a charm! Plus, it kept the kiddos from tracking dirt and water throughout the house.

As my children grew and had kiddos of their own, the tradition continued. Whenever any of the girls or boys had to go pee, they'd make a trip behind the large fir tree that sprawled in front of our house in the middle of our lawn. With so many grandkids, I couldn't keep track of who was where. The Pee Tree just made it easy when someone had to go potty!

One day we were having our annual family BBQ. The wonderful thing about this get-together was that it wasn't just family; it was friends of family and friends of friends that attended. We'd get a little fire going in our pit and the grown-ups would enjoy (sometimes too many) adult beverages and the kids would roast marshmallows. Although our family is definitely what I'd describe as laid-back and just a bit country, this was one of our classier events.

About an hour after we'd begun the festivities, my three-year-old grandson, Hayden, said he had to pee. None of us really paid attention, assuming he'd head to the bathroom; he'd been to our house enough times he knew exactly where it was. About 10 yards from our fire, I looked up to see him pulling down his pants by the pee tree, whipping out his little manhood and peeing right in front of a live audience.

# Reason #46 • Thank God, he didn't start a fire. *This time.*

## Hell's Kitchen

One morning while my husband and I were fast asleep, my four-year-old son, Nathan, awoke early. He decided he was going to make himself some breakfast; he'd seen me do it a thousand times, so I'm sure he thought it would be a piece of cake.

He got the eggs out of the refrigerator, and cracked one in each slot of the toaster, shells and all. After he popped the toaster tab down so his eggs would cook, he turned the oven on as high as it would go and put two little slices of toast in. I know he was so proud at all he'd accomplished by himself. I just wish I could've seen the look on his face when the smoke alarm went off.

Chapter 4: Stories That Delight

# Reason #47 • My kid tells it like it is, even when it's bossing her parents around.

## Don't Forget the Ice!

Tara Ann had to have things a certain way. Blame it on her mama if you will, but she knows what she wants, when she wants it….the *way* she wants it.

One evening, I'd just sat down with my husband to watch TV after getting both of our munchkins to bed when I realized I'd forgotten Tara's water. Now, in anyone else's house, this may not be an issue. But it's sure a big deal in ours!

To wean Tara off the bottle, we'd started giving her warm milk in a sippy. Gradually, over the years, it turned to ice water—and by 4 years old, we had a routine. Usually, I was the one who forgot…and was always reminded.

Sure enough, a few minutes later, my entitled four-year-old appeared, a look of "*um, hello?*" on her face. She didn't even look at me; I was the peon who forgot the water.

"Daddy, I can't sleep without my *wateeeeeeer*."

Immediately, my husband jumped up and shot me a dirty look. You see, this is a regular occurrence in our relationship…I'm always the one mindlessly forgetting something.

"Okay, honey, I'll get the water. Go get back in bed." My husband headed to the cabinet to get a cup and my little diva started skipping off to her room.

Must. Have. Wine.

  Halfway there, she hollered over her shoulder, "Don't forget the ice!"

Chapter 4: Stories That Delight

# Reason #48 • Mommy was put in time-out today!

## Mommy, You Bad!

A couple of months ago, I was having a conversation with my husband, Trey, about people quitting their jobs in this economy.

"Geeze, what is wrong with people?" I said. "They're stupid enough to give up good money just because they don't get along with their bosses?"

My two-and-a-half year old, Reece, stomped over to me, finger pointed and his lips pursed. "Mommy, you *no* say stupid ever again! That bad word. I *no* like it. You go to time-out!"

Flabbergasted, I looked at Trey who was dying of laughter, and agreed with our son that I'd better go to time-out. Reece pulled my arm, as I do to him, and pushed me down into the time-out spot. There I sat, nine months pregnant, doing time-out and trying to hold in my laughter as Reece kept stomping over, red-faced, teeth clenched, finger pointing directly at my face.

"You no say that word *ever* again, Mommy! That is a *bad* word. You know better. You sit there and I tell you when you get up. You bad. Mommy, you reaaaaaaaaaaaaaaally bad!"

Must. Have. Wine.

# Reason #49 • My daughter + drama = I deserve that glass of wine, bitches!

## Mastered Flattery

My little Lillie is very much a southern belle. She's quite the girlie girl, which I'll take full credit for since I've accessorized her in frills and bows from the time she entered this world; honestly, I don't think we've ever left the house in her three years without one in her hair. I also design a line of children's clothing and she is my inspiration for all the adorable dresses and ruffle pants that my business partner and I make.

Also, it was no surprise to see Lillie's dramatic side as she grew into a toddler, since I'd been into theater and drama in school when I was growing up. Her dramatics showed when she didn't get something she wanted or if something didn't go her way....which in toddlerhood is often.

One day it became clear that she could manage her theatrics with the precision of an Academy Award-winning actress. She wanted to have another cookie, but it was getting close to dinner and I wanted to see her eat a full healthy meal. So, I firmly told her she'd have to wait until after dinner, *if* she ate a good dinner. Tears on cue, she threw herself to the ground and thrashed her arms as her piercing scream echoed throughout the neighborhood (at least that's the way it sounded to me). I rolled my eyes. This behavior has become typical the last several weeks.

I didn't know how long this tantrum was going to last, and was trying to decide if she should be counted down to time-out (*1-2-3 Magic* style) or just thrown into her room until dinner. The latter seemed the easiest...but first, I calmed myself with a long, deep breath. In that instant, the scene changed as my daughter realized a possible time-out was near.

CUT TO: Her eyes twinkling, not a hint of upset in her smiling face, as she said charmingly, "Mama, I just *love* your earrings!"

# Reason #50 • My reality as a mom is much different than I'd pictured.

## Reality

A warm breeze relaxed me as I entered the park under the might of tall pines. I felt the day's stresses begin to float away as I listened to the birds singing a song of a summer day. A butterfly pond peeked from around the bend, the glistening water calling to me.

"Mama! Mama! I took off my shoe!"

Wait. What? I looked down at my 2 ½-year-old who'd decided to stop following my lead and sit right in a moist patch of earth. *Lovely*. Back to reality.

So here we are. Today's outing has found us on a picnic, a hop, skip and a jump from historic downtown. This has already been one of those days; isn't it funny how when you wake up you can't tell what days are going to turn out to be "one of those?" But it was. My husband has been on a business trip for the last four days and I knew my boys were feeling it.

Our morning consisted of me pulling my 17-month-old down from the dining room table, pulling my two and a half year old off his younger brother while trying to clean my home to some degree of acceptability. I'd held out for nap-time, envisioning a nap for myself or getting some writing done. However, yesterday I brilliantly decided to buy my youngest a toddler bed to compliment his brother's big-boy bed in their shared room; and though bedtime went off without a hitch the night before, nap-time was looking like a

# Chapter 4: Stories That Delight

totally different scenario. They weren't having it. I had to get them outside! *I* had to get outside.

I packed up some graham crackers, ripe strawberry slices and plenty of *agua* to sustain us on our adventure. Off we went. This local park had been on my "to go to" list for a while now, so I decided to give it a shot. Hydrated and rejuvenated from the fresh air, my two boys and I were ready to explore. At least I thought we were in those first 90 seconds of nature-bliss. After I got Sam up and walking again, we made it to the butterfly pond right next to a picturesque white gazebo.

After a hike over a few cute little bridges, we found a little girl reading a book on the edge of a garden. Sure, she was a sculpture, but don't tell Sam that. As with the mannequins at Macy's, he was intrigued by this lifelike form. He peeked at her book and moments later, climbed up on the garden to tell her a secret. His favorite secret is just to say "bootie" because he thinks it's hilarious...and people usually laugh when he says it.

Knowing that my babes were not going to sit still for even a second, I sat on a bench and pulled out our snacks at the center of that tree-lined path. It was a perfect spot for the boys; a field of grass surrounded us, allowing for endless running and playing. And a perfect spot for mom to relax (at least momentarily) and enjoy the abundance of flowers, remarkable mossy trees, and *really*, life itself.

There are always moments that we can treasure as we go through the craziness of motherhood. We just have to be sure and take them all in.

This is it, ladies.....reality as a mom.

# chapter 5

**INtense & spicy**
*shiraz*
will complement
this collection of
stories that
**Relieve**

I've lost my mind and I'm pretty sure the kids took it.

your ecards

Buy more wine!!!

FRUSTRATION. Those intense experiences that leave us feeling thwarted, often wanting to just give up. But we don't give up; we are stronger than that. Sometimes our spicy tempers emerge or we just break down and cry. This hearty, rich-colored wine has intense flavor that promises to relax even after the most stressful, irritating day.

# Reason #51 • I had to call in sick today because I couldn't get my kids out the door.

## Desperate Times Call for Desperate Measures

I had my second breakdown of the week, and it was only Tuesday.

My four-year-old was crying and throwing a fit because the clothes I'd picked out for her weren't jiving with her mood for the day. She wanted a dress (in the middle of winter, mind you), and I'd picked out an adorable pair of skinny jeans, a pink sweater, and boots. Rather than give in to my bartering like she usually does over clothes, she stood firm. It would be a dress or nothing she told me in the strongest preschool voice she could muster. I rolled my eyes and marched out to find my son to get him dressed. I walked into his room and saw clothes strewn everywhere. My little two-year-old also had his own fashion agenda, and it didn't include getting dressed anytime soon.

We should've left the house ten minutes ago, I thought as his diaper came flying. I sighed and gave in, yelling at my daughter to throw a dress on; I really didn't care at this point. She clapped in glee at her small victory, as I silently cursed. I knew this would only mean trouble tomorrow morning.

I wrestled my son down while he screamed and writhed as I fought to put his diaper on.

Must. Have. Wine.

  By the time I'd finally found a pair of sweatpants in the piles of clothes on the floor, it was too late to find a matching sweatshirt. I told myself that for one day he didn't have to match.

  After five minutes of full-on screaming (and maybe a curse word or two), I had both kids buckled in their car seats, ready to head out. Tears were forming behind my eyes at the thought of being late once again. It was snowing and there was no way I could speed.

  Out of the backseat I hear a yelp. "Bubba pooped, Mommy! It stinks real bad."

  I sighed, put my keys back in my purse, and picked up my phone.

  "Yes, hello, Sandy. I just wanted to let you guys know I won't be coming in today. Yes, yes, both kids are sick. Thank you, yes, we'll get some rest. I hope to see you tomorrow."

Chapter 5: Stories That Relieve

# Reason #52 • It's *my* turn to have a tantrum!

## Mommies Have Tantrums, Too

I've always considered myself laid back. I was the one in college who didn't care which bar or party we went to; I was up for anything. When something stressful happened, I'd always retort, "It's all good!" I moved across the country twice, experienced ups and downs in my career, and even endured a brief split from my long-term boyfriend (now my dear husband). Sure, things would upset me. But outwardly, I was always able to hold it in and put on a smile. Until I had two little ones under the age of two, I really didn't know my temper existed.

Call it the lack of *me-time* to veg out and watch *Pretty Woman* over and over again, the being *on duty* 24/7, or the frenzy of taking 20 minutes to prepare (going to the potty, getting dressed, the debate about whether they can bring their favorite doggie…why did he take his shoes off…car seats) for a 10-minute run to the store. Throw in the *lack of sleep*, and even the sweetest little debutante could lose her schizzle over the writing on the wall (literally and figuratively).

You know when you're having one of those days when you're so exhausted and stressed, you can just feel it. You take notice when you realize that Swiper is actually pissing you off when normally you can ignore him. You begin an internal debate over why Dora is always so damn nice to him when he's clearly a jerk. Or when you're analyzing your day and realize early on you won't accomplish half of the things you need to, there's never enough hours.

Must. Have. Wine.

I was truly at the end of my rope, trying to keep it together. I'd taken advantage of the rainy day to clean the house. My final touch was picking up all the toys right before naptime—which always leaves me with a wonderful sense of calm as I enjoy some quiet during their slumber. In fact, I was counting down to the moment. Maybe I'd order a movie from PayPerView and really relax.

As I got my two boys in their room, my three-year-old dumps an entire box of cars and planes all over the floor in one loud crash!

Enter: mommy tantrum.

"Why? Why, why—*why?!* Why would you do that?" I scream, with tears in my eyes. "I just cleaned up this whole room. We have to take a nap, you *know* this. Why would you do that?"

He blankly stares at me as I fall to my knees and start slamming each and every Matchbox vehicle back into the blue plastic container.

"I don't understand why you'd do that. Do you *like* to watch me pick up toys? Do you *like* for me to have no time for myself?"

Now, he's really lost as I'm going on about nonsense. Frazzled, I start to cry and I realize this could be terribly damaging for him to see me like this, so I grab and hug him tight, apologizing for yelling at him.

"It's okay, Mommy. *I'm* sorry."

My heart aches that he even apologized for what was such a simple offense.

Chapter 5: Stories That Relieve

"I love you so much, baby. Mommy is just tired. Let's all take a nap and then I'll get you and your brother a special treat when you wake up." I put the kiddos to bed and leave the room. I fall into the couch and cry all the stress of the day out. And then… I nap, too.

Must. Have. Wine.

# Reason #53 • The public tantrums are the worst! Could our children embarrass us more?

### Kickin' and Screamin'

I knew it was crazy having two boys within 14 ½ months of each other, but it's not like we planned it that way—though, some people swear by it, saying it gets easier with the two closer in age because they play so well together.

As I stand outside of our apartment building after a rockin' afternoon at the playground, I'm faced with what appears to be the most humiliating moment of my life as a mom (to date). Holding my seven-month-old in my arms, I watch as my nearly two-year-old throws his body to the ground, kicking and screaming, seriously unhappy about having to leave the playground. I take a breath and look up the three flights of stairs I have to conquer in order to get us all inside and then glance around the dozens of windows facing our show.

Someone is watching me. Someone is waiting to see how I handle this. Even if it's just God…this is a test on composure. I want to cry. I want to panic. But I know I have to act and teach him a lesson. This is the first real tantrum, I mean, *full-body tantrum* from my toddler. The scenarios run through my head. I could try my sweet approach and kneel down to his level and tell him we'll go to the park tomorrow, and not to worry! Obviously, my toddler will look up at me and say, "Oh, we can go again tomorrow? Fabulous! I didn't realize that! You're the best mom ever!"

Or I could tell him if he doesn't quit and walk up the stairs with me, he'll go to bed early or lose his favorite toy for a day. He's only almost two; he won't understand what that means.

Chapter 5: Stories That Relieve

Ugh! I could spank him and show him who's boss. But I don't spank… especially in today's world, in front of crazy neighbors. It's at that moment I realize my only option is to find my super-mom strength and carry both boys up 31 steps…yes, I've counted! Whose idea, anyway, was it to get on the top floor? Oh right, it was mine since I felt way safer up there…and hey, my calves are looking pretty shapely!

I swooped the kicking toddler up in one arm, and carried both boys up the stairs, getting them into the apartment in one piece. If he's not two yet, I wondered, what will the terrible twos (times two) have in store for me?

Better not go there!

# Reason #54 • Is this why my husband calls me crazy?!

## Schizophrenia? Or Maybe I Just Over *Think* It.

*A state characterized by the coexistence of contradictory or incompatible elements; one sign being a rapidly changing mood; from happy to sad to angry for no apparent reason.*

Schizophrenia. If my sons were actual doctors and aware of medical terms—this would be my diagnosis.

At least that's how I feel many times a day.

Tonight, for example. It's bedtime. We woke up at 5:00 a.m. this morning with no naps today. I wore them out at the playground for a solid hour. They ate a hearty meal of Spaghetti Os with extra meatballs at dinner, then bath, books, teeth brushing—the usual. At 7:45 p.m., I kissed their precious foreheads and bid them a good night and sweet dreams. I closed the door behind me and sat on the couch before realizing I didn't have my wine. A few minutes went by. Silence. Ah! I stood up to pour that satiny red into my glass, ensuring ultimate relaxation just minutes away.

Suddenly I hear my oldest calling from behind his door. "Mommy, I'm thirsty." At least, he wasn't opening it (that means he *is* aware there are rules*)*.

Thoughts dart through my mind. *Stand firm and say no. He'll get the idea and know you are not a pushover.* But the other voice says, *just give him a cup of water and maybe that will be the end of it tonight.*

# Chapter 5: Stories That Relieve

I give him a cup of water.

"Good night, Mommy." He disappears back into his room like the good little almost-three-year-old he is.

Ten minutes later—following a potty break, a sip of water, a clean diaper for my youngest, and a tuck-in for both, I find myself standing in between their beds. "Mommy, one more story."

A voice in my head explains that the boys shall get no more stories otherwise I *am* a pushover and this will happen every night until they're sixteen. The other voice says to tell them one more in hopes that this will be the last call of the night, and I'll finally get to enjoy my wine.

In the firmest, tough-mommy voice I can muster; "Okay, I'll tell one more. But *that is it*! No more games!"

[Enter sweet tender mommy voice]

"Once upon a time…"

This is the schizophrenia I'm talking about. I mean, can you imagine having this conversation with your boss at work…

*[Firmly] Leah, I'm really disappointed in your performance on the analytics report. You've miscalculated the numbers and your writing is quite illegible. [Softly] But have I ever told you how nice your hair smells? Every time you walk past me in the hallway I just think how glad I am that I hired you and that I really like you a lot."*

And this isn't the only instance. This happens when we're having a great time playing and laughing, and in his excitement, Luke jumps up and knocks his brother to the floor. My friendly aura is jolted and I'm forced to work up a tough love lesson I'm not quite fond of.

Must. Have. Wine.

Or when he climbs on my lap and tells me, "Mommy, I love you." Delighted, I go in for a kiss and notice he's chewing. "What's in your mouth?" I ask. He spits out black rubber into my hand. I scan the room, spying my lone flip flop in the corner, a chunk savagely torn from it. I go quickly from Brady Bunch Mommy to spinning head/pea soup spewing Demon Mommy within seconds. *Really? My shoes?*

Or when we had a fun outing at the park and we chase each other to the car, giggling all the while, and then he sneakily jumps into the front of the car while I'm buckling in his brother and refuses to climb into his seat—thus making me chase him from side to side, resulting in an I'm-over it...*you better get in your seat or...* (or what? think fast!) *or you won't get that treat when we get home.* My voice goes from annoyed to calm within seconds as I realize I'm bribing my toddler to mind. And, what treat? Now I need to get him a treat…

Schizophrenia? Or maybe it's an entirely new diagnosis…one we simply describe as Motherhood.

# Reason #55 • I feel resentment and annoyance toward my precious newborn.

## Rocky Hours

This is it...I've seriously watched every late night news and comedy show out there. Here I am, rocking my three-week-old baby; sometimes breastfeeding and sometimes...well, just rocking. It has become our routine. Every two hours, I rock and feed. Unlike most babies, Joseph doesn't go right to sleep after feeding.

As new mothers, we vow to be the best. We buy all the books, we ask for advice—we actually listen to our mothers (at least before the birth. Afterwards, we already know everything, don't we?)...whatever we think will help us to be better parents. Sure, everyone warns you—sleep now. You won't be getting any after that seven-pound angel arrives. But are you really ever prepared?

So, sitting here and rocking...I'm wondering why I can't take it. Wondering why I want to just break down and cry. Didn't I read the books? Didn't I heed the warnings? It doesn't matter. I still feel lost and hopeless, even though I'm holding the most precious gift a mother can ever receive. As I rock and Joseph feeds, I cringe from pain. I have blisters around my nipples from him feeding wrong—and they hurt. How do mothers survive this? How are my dang breasts supposed to heal when I'm feeding every two hours?

I'm still rocking an hour after feeding. Joseph's eyes are opening, and then drifting off...as if he's fighting sleep. I pat my baby's head, wanting to feel those feelings of love rush over me—but I don't. All I feel is resentment, frustration. I'm

## Must. Have. Wine.

sick of waking up every damn night, only to be exhausted the next day. I'm sick of having another person attached to my boobs, taking over a little part of me each time. I feel like I have no self; I'm no longer my own person. This small little being that we tried desperately to have for months and months has taken over my life—and my sanity. All the while, my husband sleeps soundly in his room…and murdering him only sounds slightly unreasonable.

I keep rocking as the tears finally start to fall. I'm thinking about throwing a pillow at the TV because the annoying blonde broadcaster is on again, the one with the perfect body and chipper personality. The one who, obviously, doesn't have children. I find myself envying her. She gets to go to work! She gets to have her own life! She probably doesn't have blistered breasts. *Bitch*.

I am still rocking, and I finally see Joseph's eyelids flutter, and then fall shut. He's fast asleep, and I know by his breathing he's not going to wake back up…at least not for two hours. I feel a sense of peace as I tiptoe to lie him down in his crib. However, rather than run back to my bed where I'm sure to find the rest I've been begging for, I sit by his crib silently and watch his chest rise and fall. I watch his facial expressions change as though he's dreaming…I watch that beautiful face, as still and peaceful as it can be. And that's when I know…I love this human being more than any other person in the universe.

As I walk slowly to my room, I realize that tomorrow night, I'll do this all over again.

Chapter 5: Stories That Relieve

# Reason #56 • Can a mommy get a break, *pleeease*!

## No Breaks

I do this a lot…I often flash-forward to an upcoming event, whether it be a week at the beach or a long weekend at my parents' house; I always envision these trips being mini-vacations from being a mom.

**This is how I envision it:**

Greeted by my loving and supportive parents, they each scoop one of my two children out of my arms and coddle and play with them for hours on end. This leaves me with the *free* time I once encountered as a 20-something returning home. I have endless opportunities to kick back on the couch and watch mindless reality TV shows, most of which I'm unfamiliar with now since my television set is consumed by Mickey Mouse and his entourage. When I bore of that, I can move over to the computer and catch up with some friends on Facebook (of which, I never did in my 20s because it didn't exist). There is also an array of home-baked treats of cookies, cake and cobbler that I gleefully indulge in. And after 4:00 p.m., let the adult beverages flow! Grandma and Grandpa joyously put the kids to bed after a bubbly fun bath. I kiss my boys goodnight and the whole family joins in on a good board game with laughter lasting until midnight.

**This is how it *was* last year, when I had a young toddler and an infant:**

Greeted by my loving and supportive parents, they each scoop one of my two children out of my arms. My infant

Must. Have. Wine.

decides he immediately wants his mom back. So I grab him from my father's arms and whisper to him that it's okay, he'll warm up to Grandpa soon. My mom is already in the living room showing my toddler all of the awesome toys she's bought for them. An hour into the visit, my mom starts a delicious dinner, and my husband and I are left to corral my eldest so he doesn't bust through the swinging doors of the kitchen, giving way to a land of endless knick knacks and breakable collectables. Throughout our stay, it's usually my husband chasing after our toddler while I breastfeed our baby and experience the only bit of "pseudo-relaxation" we'd truly have in front of the TV. After Grandma does bath-time, I lay in bed with both boys, singing until they fall asleep and I drift off, missing game night entirely.

## This is how it went *this* year, when I had two toddlers:

Greeted by my loving and supportive parents, they each take one child out of my arms and chase and play with them for about an hour until they are so worn out…*they* being my parents and not so much my kids. The rest of the visit entailed protecting my babies in a non-baby-proofed, two-story home with a glass table hosting four invisible corners, several chairs of which to climb upon, and four swinging doors that'll snap your fingers off if not careful. That's not counting the steep set of stairs leading to the bedrooms…and a fish pond outside. My husband and I found ourselves engaged in more of a workout from chasing, blocking and whistling "interference" than we'd ever come *close* to at our home. Even our date night, spent at the closest restaurant while the grandparents watched the kiddos, involved a consistent wonder of worry in the back of our minds, only subdued by the second glass of Chianti.

Grandma's mealtimes the rest of the week, without our booster seats from home, feature these two young bucks

## Chapter 5: Stories That Relieve

refusing to sit still for the extravagant meals my mother had worked hard on. By the third night, as my boys chased one another around the glass table screaming like wild barbarians, I caught a hint of curiosity in my father's face. I could almost hear him thinking: *how are you going to get these kids under control...how great of a parent are you, really*? Needless to say, this entire four-day visit found me excited to go upstairs after a couple of beers at 9:00 p.m. to share a full-size bed with my two children. I was exhausted from all of the attention needed to keep them out of harm's way and to be respectful of my parents and their home.

**This is what I know now:**

I've found myself faced with the reality of caring for my progeny even when I'm in the company of my own parents. It's not like my college loans they helped me pay off because they knew how stressful it was. This time, maybe a sort of pay-back, they are happy to play with their precious grandchildren, but they step back and let the new mommy and daddy handle the tough situations. That's my job, after all. Be thankful of *any* help you get with your children because the truth is—as a mom, there are no *real* breaks.

Must. Have. Wine.

# Reason #57 • I'm hungry, tired and I need to relax.

## Tears & Cheesesteak

Standing in the moonlit laundry room, I rocked him, bounced him, and did calf lifts with him— anything to get him to stop crying. Did anyone ever tell me how exhausting this was going to be? Even though it seems like he's asleep most of the time, when he's awake and crying, five minutes can feel like an eternity!

Tonight, my husband had just laid him down in the little bassinet next to our bed after a nice feeding. I thought we'd get a couple of hours of quiet to enjoy a delicious cheesesteak and watch mindless TV…tonight it happens to be "Intervention" on A&E, as it is every Monday at our house.

I'd just found the right spot on the couch, plate in lap, and what do you know, the first bite was amazing! Ahhhh…I let out a breath and took a sip of ice-cold root beer. I think I got in two more good bites before I could hear my little angel's high-pitched newborn cry. I looked at my husband as tears pooled in my eyes. My eyes told him everything. Can't I get a break?? We were the only ones here now as my mom had gone back home.

It was either him or me…

Finally…*beautifully*, my husband put his sandwich down and nodded at me as if to say, "I've got it, babe!" It must've been that tear forming in my eye that encouraged him.

## Chapter 5: Stories That Relieve

Five minutes later, (isn't it amazing what your own baby's cries can do to you) even after a diaper change, it was apparent my husband couldn't fix it. Liam was probably hungry... maybe. Who knows, really? I motioned for his daddy to bring him over to me. I tried, and tried. His fire truck sleeper seemed to keep him comfortable and at the right temperature, but Liam was still fussy.

So here I am, trying out every room in the house, every different motion my body can handle. He's crying. I'm crying. I'm starving, thinking about my cheesesteak in the other room and the couch, and the TV, and the peace. Then, finally, Liam takes in a couple of quick breaths and sighs. It's quiet. I don't believe it. I keep the motion going, checking the clock until it's been five whole minutes of quiet. I tip-toe upstairs to his bassinet and ever so gently lay him down. I've successfully survived another night!

Now, where's my cheesesteak?!

## Reason #58 • I gave into sex after an exhausting day and it better pay off!!

### Midnight Lovin'

*Really? Right now?* Did he not get my hint when I kissed him goodnight two hours ago and said, *See you in the morning?*

Yet, it's 11:11 p.m. and his face is snuggled up to my cheek, his hand gently, irritatingly, caressing my arm. Sure, I just got a little bit of sleep, but I bet I'll be up again in an hour and four more after that…while he snores deep through the night. Doesn't my need for sleep mean anything to anyone around here?

Then, my hesitation turns to interest; I ponder the idea as he kisses my ear. His hand wandering, waiting for permission to board. I glance at the clock, thinking maybe it could be fun, but it'd better be quick. He's got 10 minutes to pull this off. So I turn towards him and kiss his lips. I'm pleased; half-way forgetting I wanted to sleep through this. Oh, the fun! Oh, the *screaming? Not now.* It's our 12-month-old down the hall. Hubby whispers, "She'll be fine…she'll go back to sleep!"

Of course, *he'll* have no problem ignoring her. However, I can't. I want to jump out of bed and rescue her. I know she ate a full dinner just a few hours ago, so what if something is really wrong? We continue to frolic. My mind is now elsewhere. Can he just get it over with? I'm watching the video monitor. Thankfully, our sweet baby settles herself back into a quiet dream–or she's not breathing. Oh God, we need this to be over so I can go check on her. I sneak a peek at the clock and it's been 13 minutes! Now we're cutting into my sleep time! But instead of getting frustrated and ending

# Chapter 5: Stories That Relieve

the whole escapade, I remember he is my husband, the father to our child and I should hang in there. After all, I am woman. Hear me roar. And so I did. Then...victory!

I jumped out of bed and rushed to check our little girl. She was breathing and diaper still dry. Must've just been a bad dream. I return to bed.

Silence.

As I close my eyes, glad that I'd given in, I wonder if maybe I just earned a sleep-in trade for this weekend!

Must. Have. Wine.

# Reason #59 • This isn't how I pictured it… at all!

## My Cozy Little Dream Goes Vroom

One of the things I dreamt about most when I imagined having children was reading to them in bed, all snuggled beneath the covers, with their heads resting on me.

They are two and a half and one and a half and I'm still waiting for this dream of mine to unfold. You see, I have two boys. I started reading to each of them when they were in my belly. Now, the readings have become a part of our bedtime ritual. It was getting pretty exciting when Luke started to learn words and we'd slowly browse through a book – I'd point to a picture and he'd holler out the matching word. As Luke learned the alphabet, we'd search the pages for letters he recognized. That was the extent of our readings. I knew that any day now, with excitement, he'd want to start reading the stories along with me.

Two weeks ago, we got him a sturdy, *Cars* toddler bed (within the first hour the *Cars* sticker was ripped off). That night, I climbed into his red bed adorned with *Toy Story* sheets and he hopped in right next to me. This is it, I thought, anticipating the big moment. I pulled the sheets up over us, opened the book and began to read the first page of *Goldilocks and the Three Bears*. Little brother Zealand—hearing me reading, decided to climb up, too. How exciting! He crawled over me, his knees poking my shin; toenails scraping over my thigh. But he found a spot, and there we were. I pulled the sheet up over us and reread the first page so Zealand wouldn't miss a thing.

## Chapter 5: Stories That Relieve

On page three, the hungry little blonde comes across the porridge. Luke had turned his body 90 degrees with his feet propped on his bedside table. He was revving his engine apparently, '*brrrm brrrrm-vroom!*' as he announced he was a car and going really, really fast. Zealand was tugging and bending and shoving the page I was trying to read. He had a mission to destroy the page, not read it. I swiftly pulled the book from his grip as if I were a three-year-old on the playground, rightfully grabbing back my toy. He pulled himself to his feet and began to bounce away. Then, Luke flipped over and jumped out of bed, his elbow flailing into my chest, and snatched the book.

"No more book, Mommy!" he announced.

I was heartbroken! *My cozy little dream.*

Then, without warning, my frustration appeared.

I yanked the book back and said in my stern Mommy voice, "We are going to sit here and read this book, right now, or I am going to leave this room!" That voice is usually saved for moments when he hits his brother or when Zealand tries to scale the entertainment center. I quickly realized it would take more than a new toddler bed to sway these boys from their inherent verve.

Defeated, I looked at them, opened my arms out to the room, inviting them to run and play, and pulled myself up on the bed. I made a comfy spot and read the familiar story of a broken chair and a little girl fast asleep. In the background, I heard my sons making car noises—helicopter noises, a basketball bouncing off the wall, the sound of Zealand climbing up the outside of his crib, the click of the fan being turned on and off, then on again, and their loud, boyish laughter.

Must. Have. Wine.

I remembered some of the many conversations I'd had with my friends who had daughters. The majority of them will cuddle up for book after book after book. As I glance up, I wish that at least one of them would want to sit still and read with me…but I'll happily trade in my dream (for now) to see the joy on their faces as they play with one another into the last moments before bed.

Chapter 5: Stories That Relieve

# Reason #60 • I feel the darkness of motherhood enveloping me.

## The Dark Side

She's screaming again. How can she be awake already? I fed her only an hour ago. But, sure enough...she's screaming. I wait the dreaded two minutes to see if she stops, and precious silence will ensue...but it doesn't. I look over at my husband sleeping peacefully next to me. Of course he's sleeping; it isn't *his* night. I rip the covers back in irritation. Last night was his night, and he only had to get up twice. It's 2:00 a.m., and I've been up four times already.

Sighing, I stomp toward my three-month-old's room. I know I need to let go of this anger; she's going to sense it and it won't help the situation at all. The wails only get louder as I approach the room, and when I enter, I see her flailing her arms around, her little face scrunched up in agony.

A tummy ache, I determine, as I sit down with her in the rocking chair. I hadn't gotten her to burp after the last feeding—I should've known. I look out the open door of her bedroom as her screams pierce the air. I've left her door open on purpose, and I know I should feel bad...it's just not fair everyone else gets to sleep around here but me.

I rock and sing, trying to soothe her, but my heart isn't in it and she knows it. She screams louder, begging for my true attention. I try, but it's just not there. I'm exhausted, I have to work tomorrow, and she's not caring. I try her pacifier, which she's never really been into. She's a thumb sucker—and she's not having it.

Must. Have. Wine.

It's so dark…I try to imagine myself on a beach somewhere, soaking in the rays and drinking a margarita. Surely peace will permeate through me and into her. Not so much…she just screams louder. Defeated, I sigh and get up to close her bedroom door. I can only be so cruel and I know it. I pat her back and pace the room, back and forth—sometimes that has worked in the past.

Slowly I hear her starting to calm—the crying stops and short, labored breathing begins. She starts to relax, laying her head on my shoulder. I sit back down in the rocking chair slowly, not wanting to wake her now. Exhausted, she gives up, eventually falling into a deep slumber. Before I fade, I realize that the true darkness I feel isn't just from the lack of light in the room; it's from the inside.

Chapter 5: Stories That Relieve

# Reason #61 • My child is manipulating me, yet again.

## One More Song, Mommy

"Mommy! Mommy! Help me!" my child screams.

The blend of desperation, sadness and fear in his voice pierces my heart. Then a scream–a brutal shriek! Finally… heavy breathing in between frantic sobs. It's almost impossible to take!

My husband is lying on the couch. I'm typing away. We're laughing at Daniel Tosh's latest standup routine. Well, my husband is…I *was*. I think my chin is scrunched up in a pout; my lips downturned. I want to run in there and rescue him, but I also know nothing is *really* wrong. He's been testing us for a few days now and I keep going in. My husband tells me not to go to him. How can we be sitting here ignoring our first-born son's plea? Suddenly, it's quiet. Maybe a minute goes by. *And…*here he goes again. This time he's got his lips pressed to the bottom of his door, and tries again, "Mommy!"

My husband gets up and walks into his room. *Why does he do that!* After telling me not to go in there so confidently, he's buckling.

After a few seconds with his dad, my little man runs out of his room with a big grin on his freckled face. *He won!* "Mommy, I just needed to see you. I love you." (Nice touch!)

I explain to him in a whisper that he's too old to be doing this and he needs to go to sleep and next time he screams and

## Must. Have. Wine.

cries, we're *not* going to him. I shoot a glare at my hubs and take my son to the potty, get him in a new Pull-up and lay him down again.

"One more song, Mommy."

I give in, but it's a short one. I kiss him and as I leave his room, I remind him that if he screams and cries, we're not going to him.

"Good night, my love," I say, closing his door.

It's 8:47 p.m. He officially went down at 8:07 p.m. I pray we don't hear from him again tonight, that he'll get a solid nine hours of restful sleep. Either way, I brace myself. I know if not tonight, the battle will again ensue at some point…likely tomorrow.

Chapter 5: Stories That Relieve

# Reason #62 • My child will not go the F*ck to sleep!

## Speaking of Sleep

I know you all have heard Samuel L. Jackson's narration of Adam Mansbach's *Go the F*ck to Sleep,* a veritable transcript of many a parent in the midst of their child's bedtime idiocy.

The very clip fell into my hands on the first eve of a new bedtime routine. At no other point could I have related more. Unless that point is now…several weeks later.

But let's flash back a moment. In June, I took my first, very much earned and needed, trip away from all of my boys to spend a blissful weekend at a lake house in Tennessee with ten girlfriends, many of whom I hadn't even seen since before I had Luke, almost three years ago. The weekend was a mirror of the good ol' college days… full of laughter, too much beer, gossip and reminiscencing of a time when Hootie and the Blowfish dominated the air waves, everyone wondered if Ross and Rachel would end up together, and Drink & Drown was every Wednesday night at Mainstreet.

With the precision of an anesthesiologist arriving just when you're about to tussle with your husband in that "tranquil" birthing suite, I welcomed Sunday, relaxed and ready to return to my family. I'm sure I must've had some thoughts that their sleep would be disrupted with the brief change in our home. I didn't realize it was going to be a lasting change. Night after night following my return, my two and a half year old refused to go to bed. He screamed and cried and kicked behind his door.

Must. Have. Wine.

I've smugly watched this 100 times on **_Supernanny_**. I was better than all of *those* moms. I've got this under control, I thought. I shared my master plan with my husband: *Tonight, if he comes out, we simply put him back in his bed without a word. He'll get bored and we'll win.*

"Honey, when you have to go potty, just come on out and we'll make sure you go and then you go right back to bed."

He seized the opportunity. The freedom. Immediately. And five minutes later, he did again. And again. Each time, I did as I'd studied and without a word, I returned him to his bed. Before I knew it, almost two hours had gone by and I had lost my *me* time for the night.

This continued. Night after frustrating night, I felt myself losing. I was no longer in control. He was flat out manipulating me and my husband and *knew* it. Why wasn't this working? I questioned my process, wishing the Brit nanny was there coaching me.

I may not be able to actually use the F-word to enhance my wishes at bedtime, but you know as I picture my cushy couch and that lonely wine glass awaiting me in the next room, I sure am thinking it.

Chapter 5: Stories That Relieve

# Reason #63 • What happened to good babysitters?

## The New Era of Babysitting

What happened to babysitters? That's what I want to know. Back when I was 13 years old, I was babysitting to make extra money. The parents of the children I watched trusted me completely—even when my boyfriend would accompany me, which was the case most of the time.

I remember thinking, even at that young of an age, it was my responsibility to not only care for these children, but also entertain them. We'd fill the night with games of hide and go seek, dancing to MTV, or even baking cookies together. I'd make sure they'd eaten a full meal, taken a bath, and stayed up just late enough beyond their bedtime to think I was super-cool, but not interfere with their next day.

The first time I hired my babysitter, I thought I'd hit the jackpot. She was in high school, probably a girl just like me in my sitting days. Though I was a bit nervous to leave my kiddos, I knew how badly my husband and I needed a night out. We lived several states away from any family, and going out was a huge to-do. So, I ignored my gut and went out anyway.

When we walked in the door that night, Lifetime TV was on and blaring. We paid the babysitter a hefty $12 an hour (highway robbery in my babysitting days!) and she took off without a word. Although both children were asleep, I noticed my son's jar of baby food was still sitting on the counter, untouched. Weird. I'd left simple instructions on the counter with his spoon and bumbo. It appeared she'd ignored

Must. Have. Wine.

my list, but no big deal—my son was also on bottles, so we knew he'd live. I also noticed the kitchen was spotless! Hey, she did my dishes. Even if she starved my child…my kitchen was clean! Hooray!

The next time we went out, I made sure to explain in detailed instructions how to feed my son. He was at the age he also needed to have baby food in conjunction with milk, and he always ate at the same time, every day. He usually ate a whole jar of baby food, so I left two out just in case.

We came home, paid, and I went straight to the kitchen. Yes! The baby food jar was on the counter and opened, which meant he'd eaten! But, when I looked inside, only a spoonful or so was gone. What? *Well, maybe he wasn't hungry for a stranger.*

When I went to get a glass of milk from the fridge I noticed that my fridge was nearly empty. Someone didn't have an issue with hunger, that was for sure! When I looked in the garbage, I saw empty boxes of Nutrigrain bars, empty wrappers from frozen breakfast burritos….I was thinking…how in the heck does one girl go through that much food? But again, my kitchen was spotless!

Well, the next babysitting trip, we figured it out. She called to ask, (mid-dinner might I add,) if her boyfriend could come over. A boy?? Okay, calm down, I told myself. I used to babysit with my boyfriend all the time. It would be okay. But I couldn't shake my worry.

It would be another six months before we'd ask her to babysit again. I know what you're thinking. *Again?* Remember, my choices are quite limited since we live in state with zero family. It's not like we have babysitters coming out of our ears.

# Chapter 5: Stories That Relieve

This time, my son was on solid foods, and I knew it would be sketchy waters so I made chicken fingers and some other finger foods, knowing he could digest the food and she wouldn't have to help too much. I felt pretty good by the time I left, and when we got home, both my four-year-old and my nearly one and a half-year-old were lying on the floor of our living room, watching Lifetime TV. I noticed my son's face was covered in fuzz and sticky, which meant he'd been eating something like candy. I paid our babysitter and said goodbye, heading to clean up my kids' faces.

A few minutes later my husband came downstairs with twenty sucker sticks in his hands. He was pissed off, and quite frankly, so was I. Suckers, really? *Twenty*? *Are you kidding me*! I made dinner, I provided snacks; all she had to do was sit on her skinny little butt and make sure my kids were safe! I didn't even expect her to entertain them—no, that was beyond $12 an hour! I just wanted to make sure they ate a solid meal, and then she could plop them in front of a TV and do nothing more (other than make sure they didn't have a huge sugar high when I got home).

So, we're back to square one: limited babysitting options. I'm wondering what happened to the good ol' days, the days when we actually cherished the chance to make a dollar and took babysitting at a serious level and an actual means of making income.

Must. Have. Wine.

# Reason #64 • I had to fly on a plane with my young kids..alone.

## Kiddos & Plane Rides Equal Disaster

Okay, so I remember, *way* back in the day before I had kiddos, I was *so* not that person. You know who I'm talking about. The rude lady who cringes when you walk by them in the plane aisle with an infant—showing their obvious disapproval that you have chosen *their* plane to fly on this time.

Really?

Or, after seated, the man who moves as far as he can in the tiny seat next to you, apparently in serious fear of some infectious disease your child may have. No kidding…this is real stuff, folks. I've even had a man see me after I've been seated, groan, roll his eyes, and ask, "Can you sit somewhere else? Please don't let that baby spit up on me. I'm headed to an interview."

I have to admit, part of me wanted my precious little angel to throw up the green peas she'd eaten for lunch all over his perfect suit.

My most recent bout with flying just so happened to be on a two and a half hour plane ride with my 15-month-old and my four-year-old. (Yes, I know what you're thinking. That's not so long! But oh, let me tell you…I saw the writing on the wall.)

By myself…did I mention that part?

# Chapter 5: Stories That Relieve

*I thought, oh, grow up Trina! There're plenty of moms who fly with four or even five kids! Stop being a wimp!*

The trip to my hometown in Washington wasn't so bad. I sat next to a 12-year-old boy who appeared to have somewhat of a young puppy-love type of crush on me, or just found it amusing to attempt to help me with my two wild kids. The help was nice; he entertained my daughter while I tried to corral my fussy son on my lap.

The ride home was the real kicker. They had me and my daughter in seats two rows apart. Obviously, that ain't happening. Now, any of you non-flyers, know that this happens a lot. The difference? A flight attendant who cares…I've had both and let me tell you, the one who cares will save your bacon. Otherwise, you're trying to convince someone to change their seat all on your own, which is not a lot of fun.

After the lovely young woman helped get myself, Callie, and my son, Clayton, next to one another in new seats…the trouble began. A lady came along with her ticket that had her original seat number, one next to the window and that my daughter had been moved to. After the flight attendant explained what had happened, I offered to move my daughter to the aisle seat so she could sit next to the window.

"I don't want to sit next to *those* children," she told the flight attendant, as if my kids and I were deaf. I have to admit…bodily harm didn't seem that unreasonable at the time.

Especially when Callie asked me, "Why doesn't that girl want to sit by us?"

Must. Have. Wine.

Anger got the best of me; I couldn't stay composed after that. I answered loudly enough for everyone to hear, "Because she's mean, Callie."

Classy? No. A proud mommy moment? Not really…but it still felt good. We were held up for 10 minutes from taking off because no one else wanted to sit next to us on the plane. We literally had to move two times (yes, twice; me, the diaper bag, purse, two blankets, and two kids) in the attempt to keep everyone happy. We eventually took off…and I totally blame it on the stress and the mean girl next to us (yes, ironically, we ended up sitting next to the first snotty lady who didn't want to sit by us) as both my kids cried and fussed the entire two and a half hours.

I swore I'd never fly with both of them again alone…at least until they're older!

Chapter 5: Stories That Relieve

# Reason #65 • I survived being stuck in traffic with two young kids.

## Stuck in Traffic

I thought I'd beat the rush hour traffic on my way to my parents' house. I was 90 minutes into our two-hour drive with my two babes asleep in their car seats. As I merged onto I-66 after conquering the Washington Beltway, we came to a sudden stop.

I looked around me and saw car after car, bumper to bumper, covering five lanes of roadway for as far as I could see. It was a perfect sunny and warm afternoon. *There should be no traffic problems in this weather!* Next to me, a sophisticate sat in his convertible Beamer, puffing on his cigar. He wasn't in traffic at all; he was chilling out, maxin' and relaxin,' all cool on some island somewhere…if only in his mind. He definitely wasn't letting it stress him out. I wasn't stressed yet either…and then…my 18-month-old woke up.

He'd only slept for about 30 minutes and is never thrilled when awakened before he's had a full nap. Then, I heard my baby next. I started to panic, but remembered they were fine—just frustrated. *Aren't we all!* I tried to sing, rub their legs, and give my oldest a snack. But within five minutes, with all of my tricks exhausted from the front seat, they were over it! Both of them started wailing; echoing off one another, as if pleading with me to do something. But there was nothing I could do.

What an amateur, even after 18 months; I just hadn't planned very well. I'd assumed it would be a quick drive to my parents' house (something you should *never* assume in

Must. Have. Wine.

Northern Virginia) and I hadn't packed a full bottle for my four-month-old, and my toddler had already drained his sippy. I thought about trying to merge over and get off at the next exit because I knew my little one would be hungry soon. How in the hell could I merge my car over four lanes walled with stagnant cars? Really!

Just as I was about to really start crying, the cars started clearing. Could it be? We'd finally passed the accident and were free; all of a sudden, it seemed like we were alone on the road, going 60 mph with the windows down, the warm breeze calming my boys. I cheered, "Go, go, go!" and my big boy repeated it after me, "Go, go!" We made it to Grandma's just in time to feed my youngest before he really knew just how hungry he was. As we pulled into her driveway, the pent-up tears spilled out of my eyes, freeing me of that panic and stress of the last hour. I breathed a sigh of relief only moments before realizing that this is quite possibly what every road trip with young boys will be like…or worse!

# Reason #66 • I can't believe some mothers…or their spoiled-rotten kids. Really?!

## Spoiled Rotten Meanies

It breaks your heart to see your child face the harshness of the world we live in. Though it's true that most people are good at heart, everyone comes from different upbringings and even though we may practice empathy, good manners and just general kindness, this isn't always the case with others.

We were on our family vacation to Kiawah Island in South Carolina. My five-year-old son was really pumped this year. He loves the water and just couldn't wait to dive in. It didn't matter if it was the beach or the pool. He was ready for it all! My three-year-old daughter was also pretty excited, so as soon as we checked into our condo, we threw our suits on and headed down to the pool.

Late afternoon, only a few families were still there. Many, I presumed, had gone in to shower and get ready for a dinner out at one of the island's divine restaurants. As Ben ran over to the pool's edge, I could see him admiring the many floats in the water. I kicked my flip flops off and followed my little girl into the warm pool, keeping an eye on Ben as he jumped in.

Immediately, he started a conversation with one of the little boys in the pool who appeared to be the same age. After the "what's your name" and the "where do you live" get-to-know-yous, my son boldly asked if he could borrow his float.

Must. Have. Wine.

He even said please! I was playing with Lillie, but proudly watching my son.

"No!" the boy snapped, and in one manic swoop, he tossed his prized possession out of the pool and it almost landed on his presumed mother's feet. She looked up, then back down to her book. The boy glared at my son as if to say, "I will not share my wonderful toys with the likes of you!"

Horrified, I wanted to hug my baby and protect him from this savage preschooler. Clearly stunned, Ben swam off and quickly found another kid to play with.

When we were leaving, Ben said to me that he didn't understand why the boy wouldn't share his toys because *he* always shares—which is true. I was at a loss for words…and let me tell you, that doesn't happen often! I wanted to say that some mommies don't teach their kids to share and they are spoiled brats! But I refrained. I just told him I wasn't sure and that it wasn't very nice.

While my kids were sleeping, I dutifully walked to the local beach store and bought the most giant dragon float I'd ever seen, even after being coached by my husband on the drive down that we were on a budget—*no frivolous buys*. I couldn't help myself. It wasn't until I was leaving the store, I realized I had to carry this thing all the way back to the condo. So there I was, in my cute sundress and glasses, walking down the palm-lined street, hoisting a blowup dragon over my head, smiling sheepishly at the tourists driving by.

The next day, the same boy came through the pool gate and immediately spotted our awesome dragon. He came over and told Ben he wanted to try it out. Being the nice guy he is, Ben allowed him to borrow it and within minutes, the kid was acting like they were BFFs…the same dude who didn't want anything to do with my son just the day before. I was fuming!

## Chapter 5: Stories That Relieve

Just then, Ben yelled across the pool to me (so loud that everyone there could hear, including the boy's mom), "Mommy, Chase wants to be my friend today; he isn't being mean anymore! I guess he *did* learn to share."

It was all I could do not to burst out laughing as I stole a look at Chase's mom to try and catch her reaction. I figured if *that* didn't send his mom a message, nothing would.

Must. Have. Wine.

# Reason #67 • You try taking two kids under the age of three into a public bathroom!

## Just Another Balancing Act

Hands down, one of the hardest things I've ever done as a mother was taking my daughter, Lucy, to the public bathroom at the park for her first "potty outside of the house" experience. My mission–keep her and my 12-month-old son, Liam, from touching anything!

Balance is the key. First of all, do the designers of these stalls ever consider a mother with more than one young child? These stalls maybe fit *one* adult. Maybe. To entertain an adult and two small children is an act of balance…especially when you don't want their pristine parts touching anything whatsoever in a nasty bathroom stall.

So there I was—barely achieving fitting into the germy cubicle, trying to hold up my infant while squatting, and helping my precious daughter sit still on the thin potty paper thankfully provided by the park service. While she tries to balance herself, Liam is trying to grab the potty seat or the toilet paper…or the floor.

By then, I was pretty impressed that my endurance was that good, thinking that if it were a challenge on **Survivor**, I'd obviously win. But the ante is upped. Now she must be wiped. I decided to trust my princess to handle it if I could rip her a few squares. I did, and she did.

I somehow pulled Liam and myself up to a standing position using muscles I wasn't aware I had anymore and assisted Lucy to her feet so we could pull up her panties

# Chapter 5: Stories That Relieve

under her adorable little lady bug skirt. Free from the muggy cell, I wiped the three of us down with my stash of Wet Ones. Mission accomplished–*this* time.

I feel bad for considering it—even for a second, but I'm thinking diapers were *so* much easier!

Must. Have. Wine.

# Reason #68 • My kids are attached to me almost 14 hours a day, literally!

## Magnetic Legs

My boys have left me on the couch to play with a truck or dunk a basketball. I see my "out" and sneak four feet away to the computer which sits on our breakfast bar; I stand and type away. Most of the time, not even 60 seconds goes by and my youngest toddler is poking me. "Up, Mama!"

I give in and pick him up, thinking I can hold him on my hip like I did when he was 10 months old and he'll be content. No. He wants to type, or rather, bang on the keyboard. Or press a button. Or reach... reach for my diet root beer. Or feed the fish. So down he goes, and runs off to chase his older brother. I try to refocus on the task at hand. Was I checking my bank statement or writing a post on Facebook?

I feel a pinch on my butt. He's back. Of course I can't ever get anything done! So I participate in a new trick that occupies him for a good two minutes. I lift my right leg up in a ballet-type pose and rest it on the arm of our toddler-ized couch. This allows my left leg to act as a pole upon which my little boy holds onto and circles round and round and round, thoroughly entertained. Alright! I finished an e-mail. *Score*! His older brother sees this fun from across the room and joins in. Before it ends with the two knocking heads, I've balanced my budget. I'm excited I'm taking care of biz-niss! This is the longest stretch of time I've had since last night when they went to bed. My two and a half year old is now tugging at my

# Chapter 5: Stories That Relieve

pants, the drawstring coming loose and the waist band is way past my behind.

My son laughs. "I see your bootie!"

I pull them up and corral them into the living room for some dancing. With Madonna or the Black Eyed Peas on the TV, we have fun, twirling and laughing. They soon get distracted and move on to their Jeep. I'm quick to take advantage and jump up to get some work done.

As though my legs are some sort of magnetic force that neither of them can stay away from for too long, my oldest decides to use his latest technique to get my attention as he rams his whole body into my leg and pushes me like I'm a tackling sled on a football field (if this is the sport he ends up excelling in, I'll retract my annoyance with it). I hold onto the counter top with one hand, while I continue to use the mouse with my right. I'm leaning in what I'm sure is some great yoga pose, before hearing him tell me he did something sweet to his brother and thus deserves candy as a treat. "*No!*" he shouts at me in the deepest voice he can muster when I refuse him candy and stomps off.

Just as I'm about to finish typing my last sentence, my little man is right below me, both arms wrapped around my knee, "Jooss," he says with adorable, needy eyes. I sigh and decide to call it a day; grabbing his juice and joining him and his brother in the living room for some snuggling and cartoons. There's no guarantee, but at nap-time, I'll try again.

sweet & light
*white zinfandel*
will complement this
collection of stories that
indulge

chapter 6

MUST. HAVE. Wine.

For those sweet moments that truly touch your heart, join us with a glass of this off-dry to sweet white wine that never fails to satisfy the taste buds. With hints of cherry and citrus, indulge in a glass and leave your troubles at the door. Tantrums and sass are quickly forgotten with these light and tender tales.

Chapter 6: Stories That Indulge

# Reason #69 • We just had the best day together!

## Their Happiness In Our Heart

If only you could package that look on your child's face, the sparkle in their eye, those moments when you just know they are genuinely happy.

I see it in my son's eyes when he conquers the challenge of taking something apart then skillfully reassembles it. That pride when he pulls himself up on the edge of the pool after finally swimming free from his floaties.

I feel the exhilaration in his little hand gripped in mine while we're dancing to some 80s hair band I remember rocking out to on my Walkman in middle school. The glee which emerges in his smile as we watch **Yo Gabba Gabba**—glancing at one another in anticipation of the knock-knock jokes he has memorized. I see it in his whole face when I put down the vacuum to sit on the floor and work on a puzzle with him. Or, the rare moments when he shares a toy with his brother, knowing I'm watching and proud.

While lying with me on the couch just before nap-time, it's the peaceful look that paints his face. Or the chuckle that escapes his lips when his brother does something amusing – something that probably would only be *that* hilarious to another toddler. Or the wicked smile he flashes when he thinks he's tricked me into giving him another piece of candy.

Must. Have. Wine.

The quiet "I love you" as he squeezes his stuffed doggy to his chest while I tuck him in after a big fun day.

Come to think of it, maybe his happiness *is* packaged. As a memoir in my heart.

# Reason #70 • I wish I could turn back time…

## One Day They'll Be Big Enough

When Nathan was about two-and-a-half, we moved into a new house. His room had a window, which he loved to look out, but wasn't tall enough to reach. I remember him constantly asking me to pick him up so he could see outside, and it never crossed my mind that he'd ever be big enough to see out of that window by himself.

Sometime after Nathan turned four, I was walking by his room and there he stood, looking out that window. I immediately started bawling—wondering…where did the time go? It seemed like just yesterday I was hoisting him up, thinking I'd continue doing so for eternity.

I suddenly thought about all those times I'd ignored him tugging at my pant leg, wanting to play—just so I could get the dishes done. Or when he'd want me to spend five minutes coloring with him before dinner….but no, I had cooking to do. Or when he was begging me to help him put that puzzle together, but I was too busy folding laundry. All those moments I missed because I was too worried about everyday life.

One day, your kids *will* be big enough to look out that window. The cooking, the cleaning…it all can wait. Don't let your child's life pass you by; enjoy those precious times with them while you still can.

## Reason #71 • Memories made today will never be forgotten!

### Bedside Manner

This was my second official visit with this browned-haired Charleston-area doc. Luckily, I didn't have to disrobe or even put on a gown. I thought it was strange that he laid me on the floor, though he did offer a pillow. He proceeded to inspect my head, neck and arms. A very kind soul, he kept rubbing my forehead and telling me it'd all be alright. Honestly, I didn't know anything was wrong.

"Does your penis hurt?" he asks.

"I don't have a penis. I'm a girl."

"You do," he says, matter-of-factly. "Everyone has a penis."

"No, girls don't have penises."

"It's okay," he assures. "You'll feel better soon. There's a machine right here." He then covers me with a blanket and pulls it up under my chin. He reaches across me to pull up the blanket, inadvertently choking me with his elbow several times.

"You need to cooperate," he instructs.

*I thought I was.* Then I wondered where he learned that word. Cooperate.

He gently touches my cheek. "Awww. You'll feel better soon. I'm a doctor."

# Chapter 6: Stories That Indulge

I'm holding back my hysterics now, with a few chuckles slipping out.

"Don't cry. You will be okay." He kisses my cheek and then one eyelid. "I love you, Mommy. I'll be your doctor *every* time."

Must. Have. Wine.

# Reason #72 • There's nothing like sibling rivalry…except sibling love.

## A Story of Sisterly Love

Katrina had been the loving sister for her brother's entire life. She'd followed him around since birth, holding and loving on him every chance she had. Nicholas crawled around after her like she hung the moon. I tried to monitor the relationship whenever I could; if I turned around for a second too long, Katrina would be attempting to feed him a bottle by herself, or drag him around by his leg. It didn't matter; if I wasn't watching, she was mothering.

With them only being a little over a year apart, I was one busy mommy. And being one busy mommy also meant I was lacking sleep. Once Nicholas was six months old, I decided to put him in his own room, and move Trina to her big sissy's room. Eventually, we made the move happen, and the first night sleeping in my room with no kiddos was almost reason enough to celebrate.

I'd just dozed off when I heard what I thought was a little pitter-patter of footsteps. Of course, lacking sleep and assuming I was delusional, I ignored the sounds and continued to try and snooze. Soon enough, I felt my husband thumping my arm and mumbling, "Someone is up."

He rolled back over and was snoring within a second. I pushed myself out of bed and tromped to the door. Why did I have to get up to investigate, anyway? I'd have to be up in another two hours to breastfeed! Couldn't a mother catch a break? As soon as I reached our bedroom doorway, I stopped

# Chapter 6: Stories That Indulge

dead in my tracks, caught by what I saw. Were my sleepy eyes playing tricks on me?

Trotting down the hallway was my nearly two-year-old daughter, carrying my baby boy by the neck. Katrina had been walking since she was nine months old and was hauling poor Nicholas like he was a sack of potatoes. I realized my poor son was possibly not breathing, and rushed to his aid, but of course, Nicholas was fine. Katrina stomped back to her room, merely irritated that I'd ruined her evening excursion.

We put child-locks on the door handles to avoid a similar situation in the future; however it wasn't long before she figured them out and was breaking into his room at night. Five years later I still catch her from time to time snuggled up with her brother in his bed; whether she had a bad dream that night or just felt safer with him by her side —I couldn't keep the two of them apart for long.

## Reason #73 • Bedtime prayers can be so sweet…and sometimes funny.

### Dear Lord

Every evening, after bath and story time—we have prayer time. I'd pray for our family's safety, prosperity, my thankfulness to God, and whatever else moved me that day. Then, it would be Callie's turn to pray. It was a consistent trend we tried to weave into our nightly routine, and it would always be neat to see what Callie would pray for each evening.

The tricky part was keeping her in her own bed *after* the prayers were done and the lights went out. She'd sneak out of her room as soon as she heard us get in bed…begging to be able to sleep with us. When she turned two years old, she started having nightmares and was fearful of monsters. So, the new battle was getting her to sleep in her own bed began, and we did everything from bribing with toys, to punishment, to even the dreaded putting her back in her own bed, kicking and screaming (ten times). It was a fight, but we kept at it and started to see some improvement.

One particular night I was praising Callie on how well she'd done. For an entire week, she'd slept soundly in her bed with few middle of the night stirrings. We read our book of the night, "The Elephants Child," and then started our prayers for the evening.

"Dear Lord, I thank you for our many blessings you've given us…" I began as Callie squeezed her eyes shut and listened. I finished with, "And I thank you for us all sleeping soundly and peacefully in our own beds. Amen."

# Chapter 6: Stories That Indulge

Then it was her turn, which was the part we both anticipated the most.

"Dear Lord. I thank you for my baby brother. And I thank you for me sleeping in my mommy's and daddy's bed tonight. Amen."

Must. Have. Wine.

# Reason #74 • There are no worries, just ask your toddler!

### No Worries

Audrey is three, that age where she picks up everything. One cute phrase she remembered was *Hakuna Matata*, a Swahili saying meaning "there are no worries," as most may recognize from **The Lion King**. My husband and I would always crack up laughing when she'd say it, especially when she used it in the right context.

I was away running errands one afternoon, while my helpful husband watched Audrey and did chores around the house. He'd washed every bit of laundry, and was upstairs folding it with Audrey. She enjoyed helping out, and even though it was more like hindering, we let her do it anyhow. As soon as Jeff got one full load folded and squashed into a laundry basket, the phone rang and he had to leave it at the top of the stairs. When he hung up, he heard a crash, and the empty basket bounced off the last stair at his feet.

Jeff walked around the stairway and looked up at the mess of clothes strewn down the stairs. At the very top, stood Miss Audrey with a guilty smile on her face. "*Hakuna Matata,* Daddy!"

Chapter 6: Stories That Indulge

# Reason #75 • I'm amazed that such a young being can understand the importance of giving!

## A Giving Heart

One morning I was dressed for the day and Reese was hanging out with me in my bedroom. I'd turned on the TV to *Good Morning America* where they were showing coverage of the devastation of the deadly tornado outbreaks in Alabama. I noticed that Reese had become very quiet and had a concerned look on his face, watching the television as though his favorite cartoons were on.

After a sad interview with a bruised and injured survivor, Reese looked up at me and said, "Mama, we need to help those people."

Such sweet words to come out of such a tiny little person. It made me so proud that he felt compassion and a sense of urgency to *want* to do something. I guess all those times that I've tried to teach him about how we treat others was starting to sink in. It made me realize what is truly important in life…not running late to the play date, not being concerned that they eat every veggie on their plate—but ultimately being a good person and showing our children how to do the same.

Must. Have. Wine.

# Reason #76 • I wish I could take their pain away, but I can't this time.

## To Take Their Pain Away

Holding an icy pack of frozen peas to his swollen little foot in the palm of my hand, I didn't care I wasn't sleeping anymore; I just wanted him to feel better. It was a little after midnight, and he'd gone to sleep with a fight, complaining that his foot was itching from that afternoon's fire-ant sting. He hadn't complained about it since it'd happened, so I didn't think to give him any Ibuprofen before bed or even put any hydrocortisone on it. He's had three other fire ant bites since we moved to South Carolina and it's always been under my husband's watch—not to point any fingers! And, each day had been followed by a really long night of him not being able to stop scratching, thus, not easy to settle back into sleep.

This time, it had happened while he was with me at a work event I knew I shouldn't have brought my sons to in the first place. But I did, and here we are at 1:00 a.m. I'd only been asleep a few hours to his six hours. As he cried out, I gave him a sippy of milk and turned on *Diego* to distract him.

The poor little guy wanted to sleep so badly. He also wanted to itch his foot really badly. He was begging me to make him feel better. That's my job, after all—and he knew that. Sure, my cuddles probably felt nice, but it sure wasn't helping him to forget the burning in his foot.

Desperately, I grabbed my iPhone and Googled "ant sting itch help" which led to a site of home remedies. Maybe a bee sting is close to a fire ant sting? I hoped. The author of the

## Chapter 6: Stories That Indulge

site recommended everything from toothpaste to a blend of vinegar, meat tenderizer and baking soda. I tried it all…and then waited ten minutes between to see if he felt better, to see if he'd fall asleep. But he didn't. Finally, I tried Ben-Gay. It just hit me that a manager of mine had once mentioned using this on an ant bite. It seemed to soothe and he sunk into the couch, relaxed.

As I sat holding his tiny foot and brushing his dark brown hair with my fingers, I didn't care that I was wide awake. I just wanted him to feel better. I told him I wished I could take his pain away, and I would if I could. I knew this may be the first, but it sure wouldn't be the last time I'd want to protect this precious being from pain and feeling utterly helpless as a mother.

Must. Have. Wine.

# Reason #77 • I couldn't even get mad, it was so funny!

## Let Them Eat (Blue) Cake

Have you noticed that kids are more apt to misbehave when parents are occupied with something else? We had guests over one night and Leah, age three, was playing in her bedroom with her little friend, Juanita. The two girls had been born a week apart; in fact, I'd met Juanita's mother in childbirth class.

Earlier that day, I'd baked and decorated a Cookie Monster cake for Leah's birthday, and invited Juanita's parents over to celebrate both girls' birthdays with us. So, there we were—me, Frank, Ann and Rich, playing cards. I got up to go into the kitchen to get fresh drinks. As I opened the fridge door, I happened to glance at the cake on the counter. And my heart dropped.

Poor Cookie Monster had been stripped clean of his blue icing. Well, almost clean. Several tiny little fingers had raked tunnels through what was left of stringy blue frosting fur.

"Ann," I called out. "Could you come in here a minute?"

She stepped into the kitchen, her gaze questioning. I pointed to the cake. She looked at it and then at me, eyes wide with shock.

Speechless, we just stared at each other. And then I began to laugh. She joined in, and pretty soon, we were holding onto each other, laughing so hard, we could barely stand up. The

# Chapter 6: Stories That Indulge

men, hearing the commotion, came into the kitchen, and stared at the dilapidated cake.

"Let's go find those little rascals," I said, motioning for Ann to follow me up the stairs. From her room, I could hear Leah and Juanita giggling and chatting, as three-year-olds do, with absolutely no connection to what each other was saying.

I stepped into the threshold, and two little blue faces looked up at me. It was everywhere—blue icing in their hair, on their cheeks, around their mouths, on their blue-tinged little hands. Two sets of guilty brown eyes stared warily at us. And Ann and I were off again—shrieking with laughter.

The girls, realizing they weren't in trouble after all, grinned at us.

"Mommy," Leah piped up. "Can we have cake now?"

Honestly, who could be upset at that?

Must. Have. Wine.

# Reason #78 • Plain brilliance coming out of my kid…

### But I'm Smart Too!

In today's society, it seems when you're blonde-haired and blue-eyed, you're already a step ahead in our world. Being a dark-haired, brown-eyed girl, I can promise you this doctrine seriously annoyed me. When I had a baby girl that looked exactly like what every fashion magazine and TV-show focused on, I was forced to change my opinion. She was beautiful! And not just because she had light hair and aqua eyes, but because her personality spoke even louder than her looks.

Before Angela could even talk, she was sincerely concerned about those around her. If she saw me crying or even if I looked sad, she'd crawl (or later on, waddle) over to me and pat my leg or my back. When people would want to hug or love on her, she'd shy away and try to draw attention to something or someone else that needed the attention more. It was within her I found her true beauty.

As she got older, she grew even more beautiful. And trust me, people noticed. Rather than grow used to the fact that her looks were above average, she shied away from it. When she was around four years old she came up to me and said, "Mommy, why do people always say I'm beautiful?"

"Well, honey, because you *are* beautiful. You are beautiful on the inside *and* the outside. And even more importantly, you are sweet and you are smart."

# Chapter 6: Stories That Indulge

One evening when we were out to dinner, a kind, older couple came by our table, and as usual, took notice of Angela. The older woman nudged her husband and leaned toward Angela, almost as if she were a sculpture rather than an actual human being. "Well, oh, my, look at her, Fred. Isn't she the most beautiful girl you've ever seen?"

Angela threw down her fork and sighed. Her response surprised not only the older couple, but also her father and me.

"I'm smart, too!" She yelled right into the gentle woman's face.

After the couple zipped off, I looked with surprise at my only daughter. I saw only annoyance and resolve in those small fine features and I knew—she'd had enough and was going to let anyone who got in her way know.

Must. Have. Wine.

# Reason #79 • I did a lot of things wrong as a mother, but somehow this turned out right.

## True Sibling Love

We all hope as parents that our children will love one another with the crazy, reckless abandon we only hear about in stories or movies. Maybe we should think twice before making this wish. You see, Katrina was my middle child, and quite possibly, my last. Nick and I weren't planning on any more kids, at least not any time soon! We decided to take a trip to Dallas, Texas, just the two of us to get some alone time. It was much needed as we had two children, Michelle, our oldest at six and Katrina, 15 months. Nick's mom, Alice, watched the two while we had our private getaway.

After we got home, I felt that feeling…I knew that feeling all too well. I was pregnant! With two kids, and one just being over a year old, I was less than thrilled. What was I going to do, other than go crazy? Like many of us moms must do, I decided to put my big girl panties on and deal with it. Nick and I planned as well as we could, and nine months later, little Nicholas Paul arrived into this world.

Nicholas was in trouble the minute he arrived home from the hospital. Michelle was happy to see him, but at almost seven years old, she had better things to do. Katrina, however, was absolutely infatuated with him. She wouldn't leave his side, sitting by me as I fed him and rocked him to sleep. She begged to help, whatever she could do to get that baby in her arms. Her early mother-like tendencies surprised us all. Instead of a jealous little girl just wanting more attention from her mama, all she wanted was to give her baby

## Chapter 6: Stories That Indulge

brother all the love and attention in the world. I think that spoke volumes about the little girl and young woman Miss Katrina was and would turn out to be.

Alice understood I needed a break and purchased the new "in" thing for young girls. A doll that cried, ate food and made a dirty diaper that needed changed. I knew this was just what Katrina needed, something to focus her attention on other than little Nicholas. Boy, was I wrong!

Grandma Alice brought the doll over one evening when I was feeding Nicholas. As always, Katrina was sitting right by my side.

"Katrina, look at what we brought you!" Alice sat down and showed my middle child her amazing find and Katrina watched, perplexed, as her grandma fed the doll when it cried, and then changed its diaper. When Grandma Alice handed her the doll, she studied it with the most serious look I'd ever seen from her. She glanced at Nicholas, then back at the doll. She made the exchange again, looking back and forth. Then, she took the doll by the leg and tossed it, scooting closer to me and her brother.

There would be no fooling Miss Katrina, nor would there be a replacement to the bond she and her brother had already formed.

Must. Have. Wine.

# Reason #80 • My kids napped today – Victory!

## Bliss to be Savored

It's 12:31 p.m. in the afternoon on a hot Saturday in the beginning of summer. I'm home with the two kids while my husband is at work. For the first time since 6:00 a.m., it is quiet. Not *really* quiet because the dishwasher and dryer are running simultaneously and I did switch Thomas the Train over to the Singers & Swing music channel. But it's quiet in here from the hustle and bustle of "mommy" this and "mommy" that. It's quiet from my two boys fighting and bickering with one another over this or that. It's quiet from my youngest toddler trying to climb up on the dining room table and then holler out "Mama! Mama!" with his arms open for me to catch him mid-air, just so he could do it over and over again…no matter how many times I said no.

It's a blissful quiet. Knowing they are contentedly asleep and snuggled in their beds. Knowing that our afternoon will be busy with friends and fun in the pool. Knowing that our evening will be bustling as we attempt to successfully knock out our bedtime routine with two exhausted boys. But for now, it's quiet.

I'm torn between napping myself and getting some work done. Of course, more housework comes to mind…but no, not today. It's Saturday and the thought of doing another round of bathroom cleanings just to see it blanketed in SpongeBob undies, towels, floaties and miscellaneous shorts and shirts…no, thank you. I'm not going to use this amazing hour or two for that (Dear God, *please* let it be two hours).

## Chapter 6: Stories That Indulge

I'm going to enjoy it. If it were later in the day, I'd have a glass of wine… for now, I think I'll pour a glass of iced tea, relax on the sofa with a book and listen to a little Sinatra. These blissful moments of mommyhood after a crazy and frustrating morning are to be savored.

Must. Have. Wine.

# Reason #81 • These are the moments where we realize how lucky we are to be moms.

## While They Dream

During the night, when the entire house is quiet except for the white noise of his small fan, his little lips are allowing such sweetness of small breaths to exit his dreaming body. His blue satin blanket is laced between his fingers and propped across the side of his face.

His long legs which seem to be growing faster than ever, are stretched almost the length of his mattress. The strands of his exquisite blonde hair (rare in our family) highlight a frame around his 18-month-old face.

The three meltdowns from earlier and the spilled juice on our newly steamed carpet—almost a distant memory. The endless account of "no's" heard throughout the day seem less frustrating now when I look down on my sleeping son.

Who is this little person? Who is this being that my husband and I lovingly created? In the madness of a day, it's so hard to take the time to visit those questions…to really take it in. The magnitude of what it is to be a mother or a father. Every lesson taught; every kiss sealed onto their forehead. Every "I love you" realized.

You are shaping who they are with every second of the day. And isn't it amazing the love that can rise above all the chaos and stress of each day and make it all so very right?

## Chapter 6: Stories That Indulge

When looking at my son, I see his body snuggled comfortably in his bed after he's exerted all of that energy; I see the depth and the magic of his being.

A child in slumber enhances the mystic delight of being a mom.

## The Story of Katrina and Leah

Katrina and Leah are strong believers that some things are simply meant to be. Their paths crossed in March 2011 after Leah's mother, Carole, suggested to her student, Katrina, that she contact her daughter. Leah had a great idea for a book, and Carole knew Katrina would be a great partner for her on the project. Together, they worked for a solid year and half writing a book, building a platform, and establishing a marketing plan for their brand, all the while living across the country from one another and **never** having met in person. In one another they've found not only the perfect business partner, but also a wonderful friendship. To date, they've still never met in person…but are anxiously awaiting the perfect opportunity to do so.

Visit their website at www.must-have-wine.com for more real-life mommy moments, tried and true deliciously healthy recipes from The Anti-Chicken Fingers Movement, weekly MomAhas! (Motherhood tips that will change your life!) and more! They tweet @musthavewine and if you can't get enough you can also find them on Facebook - musthavewine!

## Meet Katrina Epp

Katrina's motto has always been, "Don't tell me the sky's the limit when there are footprints on the moon."

Born to a very driven father and a supportive mother, Katrina's always believed in success and never settling for anything less than the best. She recently left a career in the insurance world after eight years to stay at home with her two children and write full-time, following her passion. While it was scary leaving a successful career, she knew she had to follow her heart if she wanted to see her dreams come to fruition.

Katrina lives in Colorado with her family, and when doesn't have a child glued to her hip, she prefers to be holed up in her home office, hacking away at her computer and drinking coffee. Katrina also enjoys cooking, camping, drinking wine with her girlfriends and indulging in a little Real Housewives reality T.V.

Get to know more about Katrina at **must-have-wine.com**.

## Meet Leah Speer

Once upon a time known as Leah B,, this mommy of two sees life as one huge Saturday Night Live skit. She can see the ridiculous in almost anything. She claims that it's the basis of her sanity after surviving two big moves out of state in two years with her husband and two boys under the age of three.

Oprah Winfrey once said, "Making a different choice gives you the opportunity to live a different life." One spring afternoon she chose to write rather than indulge in a blissful nap while her boys were sleeping and that's when she knew she must follow her passion for writing. It's in her blood after all; her mother, Carole Bellacera, is a talented published author.

When Leah isn't saying something random to get a laugh from her friends and family, she enjoys movies, running, cooking, golf, going out with her girlfriends, and though you can often find her relaxing with an ice cold Sam Adams, a nice glass of Chianti is her true delight.

Get to know more about Leah at **must-have-wine.com**.

**COMING SOON**

**BY KATRINA EPP & LEAH SPEER**

---

**MUST.HAVE.FOOTBALL.**

Daddy's Favorite Ways To ~~Escape~~ Unwind

**MUST.HAVE.WINE. Vo.2**

The Wives' Edition

For more information about

**Must. Have. Wine.,**

please visit www.must-have-wine.com.

Made in the USA
Lexington, KY
13 December 2012